... to inject fairness and respect into the workplace and create environments where leaders help people to relate to each other, customers, and their *work, to progressively increase their competence and capability, and also to enjoy the level of autonomy needed to produce fulfilment and great results.*

—Jim Mather, Chairman, Gael Ltd

David has put together a very interesting book that both provides the means of raising our game of leadership in business and other organisations and challenges us to do so, not just in our home city of Glasgow but beyond. I found a wealth of ideas relevant to the needs of leaders wanting to lead their organisations in a truly enlightened and empowering way. For its future success, a city of enterprise undoubtedly needs leaders of the quality and agility and wisdom this book will help create. David has a keen eye for cultural issues too and what's needed to address them. Expect your assumptions to be challenged!

— Stuart Patrick, Chief Executive
Glasgow Chamber of Commerce

This is a book rich with profound insights and calm intelligent reflection, coupled with robust analysis. I loved all the quotations peppered throughout the book. It contains a unique, flowing blend of ancient and contemporary wisdom, packed full with challenging and uplifting thoughts and concepts: "Are you following your parents' map?," "set yourself free," "be free of limitations," "excellence is not an act, but a habit"... I enjoyed the easy, conversational tone of the writing—almost as though David were sitting alongside me in the same room. Overall, it clearly demonstrates every leader's need for both power and love, as personified by Nelson and referenced by others—balancing the tangible and the intangible and discussing the un-discussable—an inspirational read.

— Gill Gray, Business Development Manager
CeeD Scotland

David Fraser has sought to condense the accumulated wisdom of many years of study and practice in and around leadership. The result is a book full to the brim with ideas, insights, and provocations. If you don't come away from reading this with the desire to try something a little different in your own leadership practice, it won't be for the lack of new ideas.

— Professor Robert MacIntosh
Head of School of Management and Languages
Heriot Watt University

I found David's book thought provoking and enlightening. I liked the emphasis on the wisdom needed in leadership, not least the ability to admit to not having all the answers. David combines broadly based and well-informed thinking with a practical approach. This is highly relevant both locally and internationally.

— Andrew Fulton, President
Scottish North American Business Council

David's advice is practical, insightful and entirely useable, which is exactly what leaders are looking for in a book like this. The content is very readable and is actionable from the start, perfect for busy leaders in ever more complex organisations. We can all easily learn from David's experiences and advice as the thing we all have in common is our humanity.

— Abi Mawhirt, Head of Organisational Development
Dundee and Angus College

I have enjoyed reading David's well-researched, engaging, and insightful book. What he says resonates strongly with attributes Ceridian values such as being authentic, transparent, and adaptable. There is much on offer here in the way of models and structured approaches to help an organisation—and an individual leader—develop high-performing people, build teamwork, and foster a culture of genuine accountability.

— Doug Sawers, Managing Director
Ceridian UK & Ireland

Gem, after gem, after gem—I loved it! Throughout the book the author puts into words issues that have often frustrated me but I could not articulate like "being truly human seems to disqualify us from a fully professional or business career." There is lifelong learning in this book. Challenging the notion of "it's just the way I am" and giving the responsibility for our behaviour firmly back to us is simultaneously terrifying and wonderfully empowering. It's bold to defend the intangible and state that it has real meaning and purpose. Parts of the book were surprisingly spiritual for one who has no religious message. At times the subject matter is profound, introducing the idea of "self" and discussing the "soul." Being able to explain these concepts so eloquently is inspiring.

— Dr Elaine Marley, Research & Development Manager
R-Biopharm Rhône Ltd

I enjoyed reading The Mastery of Leadership. *I like its approach of initially focusing on developing and improving the inner self before then working outward to reach others. David Fraser has included several little templates or formulae that guide the reader in easy steps to self-improvement. Examples are drawn from a wide range of subjects such as astronomy, history, philosophy, and quantum physics. These are topics that perhaps don't often feature in business books, but they add to the reading and learning experience. It is an easy read and I recommend this book.*

— John McDougall, Chairman of Safehinge Ltd and
Chairman of CeeD Scotland Ltd

Dr Fraser "gets it" in terms of all aspects of leadership and relationship mastery. In this deeply thought-provoking book, he has brilliantly captured and shared not only his own practical experiences over more than twenty years in hard-edged industry, but a further decade of relevant research from sport, business, and life on the subject, taking our current thinking to the year 2020 and beyond. Not everyone has the same starting point; many are distracted by life's challenges, but if there's a possibility that you have talent within, you really should identify it and use it.

— Donogh O'Brien, Director, Aspen People Ltd

The Mastery of Leadership *is a book that not only helped me understand how to be a better leader in the workplace, but how to be a better leader in my home. It takes you on a journey of acquiring a deeper wisdom that calls you to a higher purpose in life and in leadership. It helped me understand how my personal faith impacts my ability to lead.*

— Amy Tippins, CEO-RTL Digital Media, LLC

Dr David speaks with complete authority on the subject of the mastery of leadership in handling change and growth. His latest book sets out the powerful ideas underpinning the transformational work he does helping leaders to truly lead using well-researched approaches that work. I find the person totally congruent and the book highly compelling, as it challenges preconceptions and gives much needed clarity. If you need to lead then this is a must-read!

— Peter Thomson, "The UK's Most Prolific Information Product Creator"

This book is less of a "how to do leadership" and more of a "how are you thinking about leadership" resource. It's a book that stimulates reflection and challenges thinking and one that will tempt the reader (and certainly this reader) back between its covers time and again to savour the questions it poses. In a changing world, "leaders" need to evolve and change, and this book is an excellent tool to support this process. Having read it, I am now looking forward to going back to the start, to see what further treasures it holds!

— Florence Madden, NLP Master Trainer and Executive Coach

For anyone who leads in any aspect of life—in an organisation, in the community, with family or friends—this book will make you reflect on how effective you really are, and set you on the path to improvement. A calm, thoroughly-researched, and thoughtful guide to mastering leadership.

— Heather McArthur, Raeburn Career Coaching

This is a profound book, yet not difficult to read. In 12 concise chapters, David Fraser clearly explains why it is important that leaders firstly consider their relationship with themselves prior to understanding their relationships with those they wish to lead. Liberally sprinkled with helpful quotes, this book will be invaluable to those who are willing to change. Reading this book will not, on its own, make leadership easy, but those who read it can change and become better leaders.

— Andrew Sutherland, CA, part-time finance director, non-executive director

David gets straight to the heart of the matter with his book The Mastery of Leadership*: You cannot be a transformational leader without being connected to you—head, heart, and everything in between. David brings together both ancient wisdom and modern thinking and weaves these beautifully with his own thoughts, ideas, and experience to present a case for a new type of leader. That leader is you as a whole person demonstrating courage, love, and compassion. For me, this book is a powerful way to open up conversations with ourselves and others about the true intent and purpose of how we lead. There is so much in this book that leaders can explore, both in relation to their thinking and their practice. I would thoroughly recommend this wonderful book to leaders and to those who support them as an insightful exploration of what truly makes a transformational leader. Having just finished it, I am already thinking about going back to do some further thinking.*

— Diane Seaborne, Speaker
Authentic Leadership Coach & NLP Trainer

This book is challenging, uncompromising, and well worth engaging with. In quite a slim volume, it covers a lot of vital territory, looking at leadership in an inspiring and practical way. If you want to change the organisation you're involved with, that change starts with yourself. There is much here in the way of practical exercises and food for thought to help you do just that. It is packed with nuggets of genuine wisdom and quotes to ponder—and live by.

— Ken Symon, Business Writer and Editor

David's writing style makes The Mastery of Leadership *an easy book to read though the ideas it contains made me reflect, at length, on my own views on, and style of, leadership. Fortunately, David's personal experiences and insights provide great guidance on how to go about putting the ideas into practice and the confidence that implementing the approach will lead to a fairer, more collaborative, and more productive work place.*

— Professor Neal Juster, Senior Vice-Principal and
Deputy Vice-Chancellor, University of Glasgow

David has written a powerful book full of grace and wisdom. It is not a casual read if you want to get the maximum from it. It requires an openness of mind and heart and a willingness to look at yourself first as you consider where you are in your journey towards leadership mastery. Very early on David alludes to what will be required when he writes, "If you want to be a great leader of other people, you need to begin by being a great leader of yourself, and that's where our emphasis is going to be. Successfully leading organisations follows from that."

He weaves together the wisdom of multiple others while returning to his theme that "leadership starts with you." It can be rightly said that he is offering his philosophy of life whereby leadership is neither attitude nor trait but rather an integral expression of core identity. Essential to this philosophy is the movement from duality and the tensions inherent in linear, either/or thinking to wholeness and the flow inherent in systemic, both/and presence. Such presence, manifested in heightened awareness of self and other, and what it means to be a whole person, positions being human at the core of his vision. Savour this book. Return to its mature reflections regularly, and you will find yourself resonating with your own higher purpose and empowered to lead masterfully.

— Gene Early, Internationally recognised leadership and organisational development advisor

The Mastery of Leadership

Presence and Practice in Transformational Change

The Mastery of Leadership

Presence and Practice in Transformational Change

Dr David Fraser

Tay Publishing

The Mastery of Leadership
Presence and Practice in Transformational Change

Published by Tay Publishing
Suite C, Milngavie Enterprise Centre, Ellangowan Court
Milngavie, Glasgow G62 8PH, Scotland, UK

Cover and interior design by Janet Aiossa
Cover photography by Great Scot Photography

ISBN: 978-0-9932491-0-5

Cover: The author reflecting on a changing world from The Clyde Arc, universally known, with a characteristically Glaswegian mixture of irreverence and love, as "The Squinty Bridge." In the background are familiar symbols of the old and the new: The Finnieston Crane, The Clyde Auditorium ("The Armadillo"), and The SSE Hydro.

For Stuart Hepburn
who had all this figured out a long time ago

Contents

Foreword

In this book, David Fraser has provided us with a thought-provoking perspective on how to be more effective as a leader in times of change. David is a Glaswegian and the timing of this contribution is well synchronised with the city's own re-emergence as an economic powerhouse, which, in many ways, can be attributed to the convergence of collaborative leadership from within and across the business, public, and academic sectors to effect transformational change.

David considers topics not often brought together in the context of leadership, and the result is all the more powerful for that. Agility, responsiveness, and cooperation via shared values are all characteristics of successful and responsible leadership.

My own experience of managing organisations—both as an executive and non-executive officer—has shown me the importance of a values-based approach. In this book, David is very much in this territory, encouraging a deeper awareness of the human side of working life as a complement to the more conventional managerial and professional systems and processes with which we are probably more familiar, and indeed, often more comfortable. Nonetheless, it is clear to me that the greatest gains can be accelerated and amplified by doing the intangible well.

As a fellow engineer, I appreciate the structured and methodical approach he takes to address the subjective aspects of leadership. These provide important insights to working with and through others and are important "counterpoints" to some of the more objective contributions we are familiar with. David emphasises, in particular, the importance of reconciling seemingly contradictory considerations and handling ambiguity in a way that creates an outcome which balances a multitude of factors, such as individual prosperity and the greater good; an interesting parallel with the notion of "global welfare" while growing individual value in economic optimisation methods.

This book provides an important resource for honing personal strength and resilience and for positioning ourselves effectively to have more constructive influence on systems within which we function.

David Fraser takes us on a rewarding journey that challenges our assumptions about what it means to be a leader.

Professor Sir Jim McDonald
Principal and Vice-Chancellor
University of Strathclyde
Non Executive Director, The Weir Group plc
Chairman, Glasgow Economic Leadership Board

To become a leader,
you must first become
a human being.

— Confucius, circa 500 BC

Preface

Learning to change

Out beyond ideas of wrongdoing and rightdoing,
there is a field. I'll meet you there.
— Mevlana Jelaluddin Rumi

Something in our human nature wants us both to be led and to lead others. We want to be shown the way, but we also want to make things better for those around us and those who come after. It seems to me, this duality stems from our fundamental human need to belong.

In the five years or so since I wrote and published a book called *Relationship Mastery: A Business Professional's Guide*, I have found that encouraging change and learning and growth on any scale comes down to leadership.

I set out to share what I'd learned about relationship skills—both professional and personal. I'd seen how some well-founded but underused ideas could help us relate more effectively to each other both individually and collectively, in any context. Moreover, I felt this learning was sorely needed. In fact, I had been on the lookout for a solution to what I saw, and indeed experienced, as a significant problem.

Writing a book seemed the natural place to start. However, I discovered that's only the beginning—in fact, it's the easy part. Once the book is done, the real work of taking its message to the world begins and, of course, changing anything isn't easy (or so we routinely say).

One particular challenge is integrating new learning with old habits and skills, especially when it comes to blending the whole human being with the "professional" person. Incorporating intelligent human approaches into organisations, and into working life in general, is where the difficulty often lies. We may feel we have to choose between humanity and process or profit, but it need not be so.

Essentially, the experience I now have to share is one of finding accommodation amongst opposites and of creating new possibilities when apparently conflicting factors are reconciled. This work is often to be done contemplatively and within ourselves.

Changing anything is at least as much about our inner growth as it is about outer progress in the world. In what is a remarkable phenomenon, resolution achieved inside tends to lead to circumstances put right outside. Though demanding, the process of leading change is remarkably simple, if we just look at it the right way.

The principles on the go here are extremely powerful. Some of them, however, require us to abandon some long-held certainties and approach things in a more subtle way. We need to change our way of being, in fact.

In working with this book, expect to be challenged.

Some ideas will be familiar, some less so. Some will require contemplation. This is a journey we are embarking on together and you may need to pause to reflect along the way. The material is organised with that in mind. Or you may later decide to return to an earlier point. The worth of a particular idea may not be apparent on first encounter. All, though, have their part to play in the mastery of leadership.

For our actions to have the greatest effect, fine judgement is required. Paradoxically perhaps, it seems the larger the scale on which we hope to influence, the more delicately we need to operate.

Governing a large country
is like frying a small fish.
You spoil it with too much poking.

— From the *Tao Te Ching*, 60th Verse

Beginning

Something immanent

Your first and foremost job as a leader
is to take charge of your own energy and then help
to orchestrate the energy of those around you.

— Peter Drucker

Leadership is fascinating, both in the sense that we are fascinated by leaders—which is why we follow them, in a way—and because the subject attracts great interest. We're forever striving to understand what makes a great leader, while honing our own ability to lead when the situation requires.

Much has been written about leadership, so it's perhaps surprising we haven't finished with the topic years ago. That's because it's a complex subject, inherently nuanced, individual, and ever-changing in emphasis. Moreover, it involves fundamentally intangible factors, and so any attempt to encompass the subject entirely in tangible, evidential terms is always going to miss the mark.

You see…

To even approach a full understanding of leadership, we need to be prepared to free ourselves a little from the academic paradigm, both to engage with the wholly practical and to address ourselves to the subjective dimensions of the subject—to get to the heart of the matter, we might say.

As well as that…

Leadership is a skill that, as individuals, we are unlikely ever to finish developing, so we might want to choose an attitude of mastery towards the subject.

The meaning of "mastery"

We need to dwell on this word a moment. What does "mastery" mean? Yes, it entails a high level of skill; something to give advantage; and also a strength to fall back on when things get difficult, as they surely will. More than that, though, mastery means an attitude of lifelong learning and curiosity, as well as a willingness to examine our own actions; to be both engaged in the moment, and as if looking on, weighing up and adjusting what we're doing and how we're being. It means constantly seeking feedback from our environment about what's working for us and what might be improved. It means having accurate self-perception. It means being mindful.

Mastery means learning to learn.

Something immanent

Leadership seeks to elicit success, and sustainable success needs deep roots. Whatever fuels achievement must at least partly emerge, rather than be imposed or directed, if it is to continue when our attention moves elsewhere, even if we might need to be demanding from time to time as a leader.

At this point…

We come to the first inherent contradiction in our subject: a tension between the top-down and bottom-up dynamics of leadership; between setting direction and allowing emergence, you might say. We need to find a way of balancing such opposing factors, of which there are many. That is a central challenge to which we will return later.

In the meantime…

Nurturing those deep roots from which success can grow in an organisation, or anywhere else for that matter, is an essential function of leadership. Leaders need to create foundations not just in the people they seek to lead, but also in themselves, and indeed that is the key.

And so the choice of a word…

"Immanent" means "existing or operating within." It's a good word for us, even if it may be an unfamiliar one, as it was to me until recently, and it has some other interesting connotations, which we'll come to later.

The meaning of "leadership"

"Leadership" implies different things to different people, and it is vital that we contend with this source of confusion. One of the reasons so much is said about the subject is that we aren't always talking about the same thing. Here we will take it that "to lead" means to contribute something to other people to help shape their future.

Will we shape your future, do you think?

More specifically, W. Edwards Deming, for example, wrote, "The job of a leader is to accomplish transformation of his [or her] organisation."

Let's think about your context for a minute...

What does "leadership" mean to you? Something to do with directing organisations, or cultivating the emergence of what people choose to do for themselves, or stimulating change and learning and growth?

Or is it all of these things?

And what's your situation? Is it a private-sector business, or an aspect of public service, or the community at large?

Or are you engaged in all of these, in one way or another?

Perhaps it doesn't make so very much difference. Much of leadership comes down to understanding human nature and becoming skilful with people—oh, and with ourselves. Sometimes that's where the hardest work is to be done.

You see...

If you want to be a great leader of other people, you need to begin by being a great leader of yourself, and that's where our emphasis is going to be. Successfully leading organisations follows from that.

The question of locus

What about scale? We could be acting very locally—or quite the opposite.

After all…

Changing the world is possible. That this is so has been demonstrated many times, by such as Nelson Mandela, Mahatma Gandhi, and Rosa Parks, for example. Surely, therefore, we can change merely our organisations, our families perhaps, and ourselves. Mind you, the leaders mentioned above all drew power from adversity and perhaps we don't have that motivation, but they also found strength in themselves, and in that respect, we have everything they had.

Most of us want to leave the world better than we found it. However, when it comes to change: Yes, we need to look on the outside; but we also need to look on the inside. To effect outer change and growth, the work we have to do is as much within ourselves as in the world around us. This is ultimately a rather simple idea, but nevertheless where the leverage is to be found.

But we'll get to that…

The human and the professional

Let's reflect a moment on our outward ambitions:

to run a profitable business, to direct a successful public sector or non-profit organisation, to lead an effective team, to be a strong contributor, to make a difference in the world, to take home a worthwhile reward, or to support a happy family. All of these compel us to be skilful in the human dimension as well as the professional domain.

And yet…

The human and the professional are not always happy bedfellows. Sometimes, the professional disciplines appear to preclude the human touch, though that is a false dichotomy, as we shall see. Other times, being truly human seems to disqualify us from a fully professional or business career, which is the reverse of the truth as well, though a widely held belief.

The thing is…

The necessity of this choice isn't real, though it appears to be. In fact, encompassing the alternatives is an essential step towards success on either front.

Wait though…

They're not actually alternatives, and that's important to realise: They're complementary factors, needing to be blended. An easy and straightforward task, though, it isn't, or it would have happened already.

Oil and water don't mix very easily. That's what I've found, anyway.

I've spent a while—the best part of a decade—figuring out how to blend these equally compelling but seemingly incompatible perspectives. Perhaps you've had this experience too: You learn something new, which you know has a great deal to offer, but it's not self-evident how to integrate what you've learned with what you or your organisation is already doing and what some call "business as usual." Often, the problem is bringing something intangible into a world that's obsessed with the tangible and the short term, with little patience for the longer-term fundamental changes it really needs.

Just because something is intangible doesn't mean it has neither structure nor energy. On the contrary, subjective experience can be approached systematically, and the intangible has a great deal of power.

As Peter Senge, an authority on leadership and learning in organisations, would say, "the intangible appears insubstantial and the tangible appears substantial, but in fact it's the other way round. The intangible is substantial and the tangible is insubstantial."

Leadership and management

Leadership and management are different things. We need both, of course. Management is about doing the tangible well and efficiently when what needs to be done stays much the same. Leadership is concerned with doing the intangible effectively when the entity and the task need to become something different.

Management draws on formal authority; leadership rather less so. In fact, formal authority may not always be an asset in true leadership.

However, leadership needs management—and often a great deal of it—to give effect to its choice of direction. Conversely management needs leadership to keep an organisation adapted to its environment, or perhaps sometimes to adapt the environment to the organisation.

Leadership is, of course, often (but not always) concerned with teamwork. We might observe that if the team didn't follow, the leader didn't lead. As beauty is in the eye of the beholder, so leadership is in the heart and mind of the follower.

Many believe management has historically been much more effectively taught than leadership. Perhaps that's because "schools, at every level, prefer to teach what can be taught rather than what needs to be learnt," as Charles Handy put it. In other words, schools prefer to teach the tangible.

Here we are concerned primarily with leadership rather than management, especially the inner journey of leadership—not just doing something different, but also being something different—in a transformational change.

It starts with you

Everyone thinks of changing the world, but no one thinks of changing himself.

— Leo Tolstoy

Changing the world, or changing just your world, or changing just you are all part of the same thing, because changing anything begins with changing yourself. This is not so widely understood, much less put into practice. As contemporary writer Jackson Brown puts it, "Never underestimate your power to change yourself; never overestimate your power to change others."

A desire to make a difference is part of the human quest for significance. The ability to lead change successfully is, therefore, sought by many. However, change is often presumed to be something to be done with or even to other people, when in reality, the only change we have any real control over is that which we undertake ourselves. Fortunately, it turns out that, to the extent we are in a relationship with the external system, as we change, so the system changes.

How does that work?

Well, the truth is...

This is a rather profound journey of discovery we are embarking upon together. Yes, we are talking about leadership, but in fact our subject goes a little deeper. Not so long ago, I was preparing to give a talk to an audience of a hundred or so business leaders and managers. While reflecting on the title of the session,

I realised I was addressing a bigger theme than I initially imagined. "A Philosophy of Leadership and Interpersonal Effectiveness" the screen showed as my title, but it might as well have said: "A Philosophy of Life."

To lead ourselves and thereby others well, we need to know our purpose and to understand life, or at least have a philosophy that makes sense. And then, we need to go first. That's not so surprising because another, rather ancient, meaning of "to lead" is to step forward or across. According to Dee Hock, that definition comes from an old Scottish dictionary, curiously.

Finding your balance

Perhaps we would find it easier to lead if we could be single-minded at all times. Unfortunately, leadership doesn't work like that.

Do you see unresolved conflict around you?

Our times require us to reconcile opposites in our lives, our organisations, and our societies. We ourselves face dilemmas: Part of us wants one thing; part of us wants another. We see unfettered pursuit of one objective causing extreme difficulty in another area—the pursuit of wealth causing unsustainable exploitation, for example.

We might like to think that we can focus on one consideration, like profit, and rely on others to make the case for its opposite, like concern for the environment perhaps. We might like to think that others will take care of those people who can't take care of themselves. We might like to think that we can ignore the need for moderation ourselves. Unfortunately, these are no longer sustainable positions to take, if they ever were, because it's too easy for one argument to dominate and for balance to be lost, as happened in the banking and economic crisis of 2007–8.

The truth is…

It's no longer viable to say: "Our job is to do this; dealing with the consequences is someone else's problem." Dealing with the consequences is our problem. However, this shift flies in the face of traditional perspectives of business, public service, and community, as well as the demarcations between them. We need to recognise at last our interdependence and handle the ambiguities that arise.

The question, of course, is how.

Complexity, simplicity, and the ideal

Occasionally, people see fundamental principles as philosophical or idealistic or esoteric. I don't think they are, actually, but in any case, if you don't have a clear view of the ideal, how can you possibly move towards it?

Even then…

Moving towards the ideal might not be so easy. We don't have complete discretion to do as we see fit in our organisations—or in our families, for that matter. So leadership needs to be seen in that context. Do you know anyone who could say that she really controls everything in her organisation? Perhaps it's true of an owner-manager of a business who doesn't have to answer to anyone, but she still has to please her customers. We may all have to lead in an environment we don't completely control, where we don't have authority over everything or everyone. Even chief executives have shareholders to please, usually, and the heads of public bodies have politicians and the press to satisfy.

So that means…

Whatever our position, we may not be able to lead all the time. We may have to do a fair bit of following as well, and some of the time, our path may involve more of a management role, implementing someone else's agenda. In other words, at any level, leadership is a complicated business. All the more need, then, for simplicity to cut through the confusion.

Our working lives can seem pretty complex, even overwhelmingly so, can't they? Sometimes, though, overwhelming complexity pushes us in the right direction because in desperation, we look for an easier way. As Winston Churchill said, "Out of intense complexities, intense simplicities emerge."

Really, the simplest things are the best. Profound, simple truths frequently allow us to avoid more complicated approaches, which are difficult to implement and rarely deliver the desired results.

However, we may need some courage to choose the more direct path.

I wonder if this metaphor works for you…

Churchill's intense simplicities are a bit like the sudden clarity of arriving at the top of a mountain. You know exactly where you are, and you can see very clearly. On climbing up, complexities of topography fall away as you reach the top. Proceed lower down, in amongst the folds of the landscape, and everything is much more involved and difficult to discern as complexity compounds complexity.

Some of the intense simplicities can be distinctly challenging, so please do expect to be challenged here. For example, we can't talk properly or comprehensively about leadership without incorporating some truths rarely discussed in conventional sources. Here, we will talk about these factors explicitly because, to be a leader, you need to understand them thoroughly—to live them, in fact. If you don't, you're "only playing with half the deck" at best. However, whether you talk about them openly in an organisation or not is another question entirely. That's your decision, but if you're not aware of their importance, you won't be a great leader—simple as that.

We can't solve our problems at the same level of thinking we were at when we created them.

— Albert Einstein

Sources

Our journey together in this book involves weaving together insights from a number of distinguished contributors—some of them classic, some of them contemporary. Whenever possible, I've gone to the authoritative sources to study most of the subjects covered. Their names may not be familiar, but they are the leaders in their respective fields. They're listed in the Bibliography, along with notes on the relevance of each entry. "World class" is an overused phrase, but these sources are unsurpassed in what they teach. Also included here are reflections on my 50 years of personal and professional experience, along with insights from a number of less well-known sources.

Blending all these philosophies with each other, never mind with the conventional world of leadership and business organisations, is a significant challenge. Nevertheless, that is the journey we are embarking upon. In many ways, this book is the result of taking all of these ideas and principles, putting them in one pot, and applying a little heat.

Or we could think of it like this…

If all these sources of wisdom were present in one room, what would the conversation be? What would they eventually conclude? Or if they were musicians in an orchestra, what piece would they be playing?

There's a stage in writing where I gather the relevant books I've read together in a box—a red plastic storage box. I know this may seem a little bizarre, but there's something significant about red: Somehow, it blends the books—about 40 of them—into a unified energy, or at least I can imagine that happening. With my first book, *Relationship Mastery*, I realised that particular energy was... actually, it'll be better if I tell you that later, but it was a profound realisation for me at the time.

The question I asked myself at that point was: "What's the unifying thought or energy this time?" If all my sources, quite a few of whom I know personally, were having the conversation of their lives in that box—between their books so to speak—what would they be talking about?

In the coming pages, I'll tell you what I heard, as best I can discern it and as it relates to my own thinking and experience.

The influence of culture

It's important to recognise the influence of several distinct cultures as we address our theme of leadership and its mastery. At the risk of upsetting most of the English-speaking world, let me over-generalise…

First is Scottish culture, which affects me most as it is my immediate environment and which is characterised particularly by a strong commitment to social justice and the importance of community on the one hand, but handicapped—in my opinion—on the other by a reluctance to embrace an enlightened attitude towards matters emotional and spiritual, as well as a disdain at times for personal success and the leadership people sometimes need. My home city of Glasgow can be particularly iconoclastic, though with a certain warmth and humour. That trait may be a key underpinning of its recent progress.

Next most present is British—or perhaps more accurately, English—culture, which shares with Scottish culture a disinclination towards the emotional and spiritual, but in contrast, celebrates individual achievement more readily and perhaps finds a different line between personal prosperity and social equality, leaning more to the former, relatively-speaking.

Then we have an American influence, which is much more open to handling the emotional and spiritual component of life alongside the everyday, or at least it has a plentiful supply of proponents of that, whilst at the same time valuing individual achievement particularly highly and placing even greater emphasis on self-reliance.

European culture is prevalent too, particularly French. Here, a respect for knowledge and technology comes through in a way that can be critically missing in Britain, but which America picked up from France, to its continuing benefit.

The Hopper brothers set out the significance of these factors in the context of leadership and organisations in their book *The Puritan Gift*.

Finally…

Among my influences—as best I perceive them, anyway—are elements of Eastern culture, particularly from India and China, which I experience as a very healthy counterpoint to the excesses of Western civilisation. I'm referring specifically to the *Tao Te Ching* (or Taoism), Buddhism, and *The Bhagavad Gita*, which was Mahatma Gandhi's guide.

All of this is grossly oversimplified, but is nevertheless an indication of what may be factored into my perspective. One might presuppose that some kind of progress would emerge from blending all of these cultural influences and others besides. That might begin to be a response to the challenge Joshua Cooper Ramo cites, quoting Ulrich Beck: "'At the beginning of the twenty-first century, the human condition cannot be understood nationally or locally, but only globally,'" because "what modernity manufactures better than anything else is new and incalculable risks that we all share and partake in, even if we're not aware of them."

The blend of cultures I reflect is inevitably partial. Nevertheless, I believe it takes us in a helpful direction.

A special companion on our journey together will be the *Tao Te Ching*, written in ancient China about 500 BC. The Tao (pronounced "Dao") means the Way, and the *Tao Te Ching* means the Book of the Great Way. The Taoist way of being is very different from what we're used to in the West, and it has a great deal to offer in the way of the balance we have lost and now need.

It's often said in the West that we struggle to make some of the Eastern approaches to management work. That's really because we don't have the personal disciplines to match: We don't follow the Way of the Tao.

However, as Michael LaTorra says with beautiful paradox, reflective of the Tao itself: "The Way is only attractive to those who are already wise enough to know how foolish they are." He continues: "Sarcastic laughter from other fools who believe themselves wise does not deter the truly wise from following the Way."

I suppose the Tao particularly appeals to me as an engineer because it has that quality of helping us see behind the superficial. It helps us understand what's really going on and in so doing, find ways of being much more effective by operating at a deeper level.

If you want to be a great leader,
You must learn to follow the Tao.
Stop trying to control.
Let go of fixed plans and concepts,
And the world will govern itself.

— From the *Tao Te Ching*, 57th Verse

Just those few lines convey so much. They do seem paradoxical, but in fact, they capture the essence of what we need to learn. Coming to terms with the paradox is exactly what will take us forward.

Our journey together

I don't ask you necessarily to accept what I say about culture or anything else. What I do ask is that you assimilate first and evaluate later. In other words, keep the evaluating and the learning separate. Try things out. As Milton Erickson said, "Experiential learning is best done when one is simply experiencing and not examining the experience." Keep the sceptic in check. Otherwise, all you do is slow down your own learning.

All that said…

Everything I'll cover is something I have found to work and work well. It has stood the test of time.

There are lots of necessary but not sufficient conditions for success—much to get right. We're all inclined to fall into the trap of pushing one idea as if it's the answer when in fact, it's only one of the pieces we need. So it's wise to look for what's right about something rather than what's wrong with it, in a spirit of appreciative enquiry.

Sometimes we might feel we don't have time to pay attention to all this. Well, we don't have time not to, in my view. The thing is, getting clear about some powerful, simple truths can save a great deal of time. "I'm too old to learn new skills," said one executive, but she realised that in fact she could do just that. The learning was both the quick way and the answer to a number of issues. We are talking about taking the fast lane here and the skills are all learnable skills. They are for you too.

Along the journey I am inviting you to share, we're going to weave several threads together: One is leadership; another is change; others are personal growth, organisational learning, the skills we bring to our professional relationships, and some deeper timeless insights. Our destination is some simple profound truths that can help us lead well in challenging times. We will find these interwoven threads all arrive at much the same point as intense simplicities emerge, to borrow Winston Churchill's phrase.

I'll also tell you about the most frightening thing I've ever done professionally—possibly the most frightening thing I've ever done, period, actually.

We'll cover what really makes the difference in professional relationships.

And I'll set out how to get organisations (and people) to learn, which can be a challenge, in case you haven't noticed.

We'll finish with the ultimate key to success as a leader, which the majority of sources don't tell you.

The answer to all of these questions is much the same thing, in fact, but let's build up to that.

As we do…

We might change your life. We're certainly going to talk about things that have changed people's lives. They've definitely changed mine. And without a doubt, they have the potential to change yours. It's a question of choice.

Leadership starts with you.

It's as simple as that.

1

Starting Points

Early wins, essential shifts

Progress is impossible without change, and those who cannot change their minds cannot change anything.

— George Bernard Shaw

In leadership and in life, we face many dilemmas and ambiguities, conflicts to be reconciled, and opposing considerations to balance.

Before we get into that though…

We need to cover certain things that are really givens. Without these, the rest of our work here won't make proper sense or be effective. I say "givens" as if these concepts are widely understood and accepted. In fact, they may well not be, even though the principles are unambiguously necessary steps in the direction of life, leadership, and learning.

In a number of areas, there is really no doubt: To be fully effective leaders and find strength within ourselves and other people, we must have the right starting points in place. To achieve those, we may need to shift our approach a little.

Of course, distinguishing between contradiction and clear choice is not always straightforward. Something we imagine is clear-cut, we may later realise, is not as unambiguous as we thought, and another aspect we believe to be contentious, we eventually decide is not in question after all.

So…

We must keep in mind the limitations of our worldview. Our "map" is just a snapshot at a point in time and an incomplete one at that. It's likely to change as we add to and reflect on our experience and knowledge. What you're reading here is, of course, merely an expression of my current worldview. I'd like to think it's a well-informed, well-researched, and well-developed worldview, but nevertheless, it's just my worldview.

Some, or even all, of the "starting points" that follow, you will have already. They may seem obvious intellectually, but the question is: Are they your actual behaviour? Are they a way of life?

They need to be.

Taking responsibility

Don't blame. All you're doing is deflecting your own learning.

I'm talking about choosing to take responsibility for what happens around you in ordinary, everyday human interaction. Holding other people accountable for their performance in a contractual relationship is another subject. You'll get better results when you choose to believe you create what happens to you, instead of being a victim of other people, or circumstances, or even, in a funny kind of way, yourself. As Wayne Dyer says, "Focus on understanding yourself instead of blaming others."

"The truly free individual is free only to the extent of his own self-mastery. Those who will not govern themselves are condemned to find masters to govern over them," writes Steven Pressfield, citing Socrates. "Individuals who are realised in their own lives almost never criticise others. If they speak at all, it is to offer encouragement." In other words, what they do say meets the Buddhist test of being true, necessary, and kind.

If you see yourself as having things done to you, well, for a start, that's hardly the posture of a leader. More than that, though, you're ceding control of your life to other people and other things. How can you make improvements if someone else is in control of you? If you see yourself as a victim, you're self-evidently disempowered. You must be: You've decided someone else is responsible for your situation.

Most of us have moments when we slip into the victim mindset, when our resilience falters. But unless we quickly return to a position of responsibility for our lives, we won't get very far. Our normal state needs to be the very opposite of victim.

We have a language issue here…

Finding the right word for the opposite of "victim" is a challenge. "Victor" isn't right. "Creator" is perhaps the closest we can get, setting aside its biblical overtones—creator in the sense of someone who creates their circumstances or at least chooses to believe they do—or maybe the right word is just "leader." If we decide we are the source or originator or even leader of what happens to us, then we maximise our chances of taking the actions that can result in a different outcome.

In contrast…

If we draw back from total responsibility and believe even one per cent of what happens to be controlled by someone else, then of course we let ourselves off the hook of choosing to do something about our lives. The very things we could act on, but prefer not to because of the difficulty, will inevitably be the ones we place in the one per cent that is "not us" or "their problem." Another way of putting this creator principle is choosing to be at the "cause" rather than at the "effect" of what happens.

One question that will take you to an attitude of responsibility in a particular context is to ask yourself, "What am I doing to create the very thing I am complaining about?" or "What am I not giving that I could be giving?"

Now, of course…

Objectively speaking, other people probably could change in ways that would be beneficial to them and us, but the only behaviour we can definitely alter is our own. That's where we have complete control.

All of this is more than a cerebral choice: Being at cause—a creator—goes with a different physical experience than being at effect—a victim. We actually feel different when we step into responsibility: solid, grounded, and dynamic. In contrast, a victim state feels shallow, thin, and static.

It helps to develop our awareness of the inner signals that tell us when we're letting things happen to us and when, in contrast, we're being a creator and taking control of our lives. What are the signals for you? How do you know when you've "stepped up?"

It might be like this…

Being in a resourceful state might go with feeling a little taller, more upright, lighter on your feet, but also grounded, having a clear voice, a feeling of greater awareness, and a sense of filling the room or the space you're in. This is an individual thing and your precise experience may be different in the details. It's possible your association will be more visual or auditory—something you see or hear—but notice the signals; that's the point.

Now…

Could you be a victim of yourself?

What do I mean? That's when we say things like "I can't help it. That's just the way I am," or "I'm just being myself," or "I would do that but it doesn't feel natural." If we act helpless in the face of our own personality, we deny our own ability to change and diminish our ability to influence those around us. If we're not prepared to take responsibility for ourselves, why should anyone else take responsibility for themselves… or us for that matter?

If we choose the role of victim, we disconnect ourselves from the levers of change. So, the first of our starting points is to choose to take responsibility for what happens to us and to have an unshakeable belief that we can change our outcomes.

Respecting values

There is nothing either good or bad, but thinking makes it so.
— William Shakespeare, (*Hamlet* Act II, Scene 2)

"Good" and "bad" or "positive" and "negative" only have meaning in relation to a set of values. Some of those might be deep-seated and unconsciously held, producing in us quite visceral responses to events, but nevertheless the sense of good or bad, acceptable or unacceptable, is something we determine rather than being a universal truth.

Shared values are rather less widely held between people than we perhaps imagine, and so habitually applying the labels "positive" and "negative" tends not to serve us very well. Clearly certain behaviours are almost universally seen as undesirable or worse, but strictly speaking, there are no absolutes. We can usually find someone who thinks something is acceptable however extreme we may judge it.

So be clear about your values, but be aware, they're just your values.

This line of thinking takes us to a "non-judgmental" attitude, which doesn't mean abandoning attempts to influence in a way that will be beneficial. Rather it means not imposing our values on other people. We'll achieve a more powerful result by developing shared values together.

Say it (and think it) the way you want it

Always express what you want the way you want it, rather than as an absence of what you don't want. You might have to think for a minute or two to move from what you don't want to what you do, but it's worth the effort. In fact, if you've never articulated to yourself what you do want, you've no chance of manifesting it in your life. Everything created is created twice: once in your mind and once in reality. Until you create what you want clearly in your mind, you won't take the actions or gather the resources that will make it actually happen. This is such a fundamental and simple and important point, but it's surprisingly little known. It's enough in itself to change the world or an organisation or a life, if consistently applied.

In stating things positively, we're essentially programming our unconscious mind to deliver what we want, and our unconscious doesn't compute a negative. It doesn't know the difference between "stressed" and "not stressed," for example. So if it's "not stress" you want, start thinking about being calm.

The classic way to demonstrate this is to ask that you not think of a blue tree, or of a pink elephant, or of your house with green spots.

But you did, didn't you?

So express what you want as a positive, not the absence of a negative—well, if you want it to come about anyway.

What you say… will be the way, or as Bob Proctor and others have said: "Thoughts become things."

Seeing system and structure

We tend to react to events. In fact, for many, that's the norm: Something happens, we respond; something else happens, we respond again; and so on, all day long—all life long, in fact. The trouble is our initial response may be counter-productive, taking us deeper into a problem state. Taking a step back and understanding the systemic nature of things can help us see that a different reaction from the obvious choice would lead to a better outcome.

You see…

A cause and its effect are often separated in time and space. An action taken here may result in a consequence over there at some point in the future. A transactional way of operating—processing a series of decisions one dimensionally in the moment without consideration for the effect of time—is likely to lead to results less effective than they could be and sometimes even a poorer outcome than taking no action at all.

A business modelling exercise, discussed in

The Fifth Discipline, frequently shows that many teams achieve less with their consciously chosen actions than results from a completely unthinking, simplistic, and unemotional strategy. The implication is that some leadership teams would be better doing nothing and leaving their organisations to run themselves rather than take the actions they choose to take. Part of the lesson is that human weaknesses tend to intervene and prevent teams from seeing what the information in front of them is really telling them, if it's telling them anything at all. Instead, we tend to see what we want to see and respond to drama with more drama.

Nature is full of systemic behaviour. For example, all sorts of plants start their growing cycle in the winter months, while it's still getting colder. How do they know to do that? Daffodil bulbs, for example, start growing roots around about October. If they just reacted un-systemically to events, they wouldn't do that.

Here's the thing...

If you don't understand the structure of what you're dealing with, you're likely to be wasting your time. Your leadership efforts will likely be ineffective or even make matters worse. For example, sometimes the way to solve an overloading problem in a hospital is to move resources away to reinforce upstream services, which reduces demand on the hospital—the opposite of the obvious action.

One benefit of seeing the structure of an issue clearly is that it can save you from expending energy on a futile purpose. The problem may remain insoluble, but at least you will conserve your resources. In *The Art of War*, Sun Tzu writes of positioning oneself in the landscape to be in a favourable position for the potential "battle" to come. That's the benefit of understanding structure.

In starting something new and perhaps daunting, ask yourself how would nature do it? Nature usually starts very small, among other things, and that could be part of the answer.

As Peter Senge would say, studying system and structure is like looking at the stars in the night sky: The more you look, the more you see.

Moving from linear to circular

In the West, we tend to have a linear view of things: Cause results in effect, just as we have been discussing. However, in many situations, it's more complicated than that: Yes, cause leads to effect, but effect leads back to cause, perhaps a little later in time, and via some other factors.

Putting it another way…

We don't have many truly independent variables to work with—levers we can push or pull without interference. Just about every factor is influenced by something else. Our attempts to influence a system by manipulating a few variables may have disappointing results. And whatever results they do achieve may well be undone in time. Other variables and feedback connections restore the entity—the one we thought we had changed—back to its original state.

So not only may we be trying to turn the proverbial supertanker, other forces will happily reset the vessel to its original course when we're not looking, thank you very much. That tendency is the norm rather than the exception.

So a healthy starting point is an assumption that everything is influenced by something else.

Showing up

Before we can begin to influence our environment afresh, we must look to our own presence: Who are we when we show up in the world?

We're often exhorted to "be ourselves" and that's good advice. The trouble is... well, there are several problems: Often we don't know who we are, not really; there are several versions of us to choose from (actually, that's a good thing in many ways); and who we are could do with a little polishing. Most significantly, we probably haven't accepted who we are, which is a necessary first step in being accepted by others.

So "being yourself" isn't the simple matter it sounds.

We can't be influential by being anything other than totally authentic. We need to be real and open. People need to trust that what they see is what they're going to get; that there will be consistency. They are attracted to that authenticity—strongly so, in fact. They will also accept what we say, or at least they'll listen. If, on the other hand, we pretend to be something we're not, others will prod and poke to find the inconsistencies, to expose the shallowness of what they're experiencing. They may well not hear us out. They will interrupt to challenge our pretences, to find out where the truth lies.

The issue is…

Being real and authentic depends rather a lot on being congruent in ourselves. In other words, we can hardly expect to come across consistently if we aren't consistent within ourselves in the first place. And that may take some work. Indeed, complete consistency isn't always possible.

So what then does "being real" mean if we feel undecided?

Well, it could be the answer is to share our dilemmas, to be honestly conflicted, if you like.

Here the gains build over time through our reputation. Others are attracted to people they perceive as real, as true to themselves. This is not something that can be faked.

Showing up authentically as a human being is by no means the norm. Many prefer to hide behind a work persona and not expose their true selves, for example. Coming out from behind that screen is not a five-minute task either. Rather, it's the work of months and years, but the reward is meaningful and productive relationships with other people and good practical results. Being real may mean being out of our comfort zone, at least until it becomes our new norm. It may mean being vulnerable for a time.

Being real is perhaps not a choice everyone wants to make, and that is a right we can all exercise. On the other hand, in an organisation, encouraging people to be their true selves is going to lead eventually to a stronger team and better results.

If, instead, we constantly abandon our personal truth, we will make little lasting impact.

The people who have sacrificed their view in order to get to the top have very often left no footprints in the sands of time.
— Tony Benn

Overcoming your own resistance

Sometimes, we feel we don't want to do some particular thing. "It's just not us," we claim. Steven Pressfield, author of *The War of Art*, would say that's just "the resistance" talking; that it's part of our primitive brain acting to keep us safe, or apparently safe, at least in the short term. We tend to pander to it, and that holds us back.

Now…

There's a difference between the difficulty of choosing from amongst options and hesitancy about action or non-action. When it's really time to act, we need to act. We need to overcome our reticence and commit to our action. At least if we want results, we do.

Often what we're afraid of is exactly what we need to do to maximise our growth and development. Sometimes, our bosses and mentors push us out of our comfort zone to do these things anyway, which forces us to learn. If we're in a more self-directed role, it falls to us alone to know when to step into an uncomfortable situation in order to grow. As Neale Donald Walsh says, "Life begins at the end of your comfort zone." If we go easy on ourselves and stay where we're comfortable, we won't progress.

Being in our comfort zone, where we are prepared to let life happen to us, is just one step away from being a victim. If instead, we move outside of our comfort zone, we take more control of what happens and occupy a creator role in our own life. We step up, or step forward, you could say.

Believing in the believable and sometimes the unbelievable

There's more to life than that we can physically prove.

— Oona McFarlane

Many of us have been trained, in a scientific or administrative way, always to look for the facts to justify our beliefs and decisions, and to act only on the basis of the "evidence." In the appropriate context, such as the spending of public finances, that's probably necessary. However, there are some matters where physical proof is beyond us, and we must select our beliefs for other reasons—principally the evidence of our own experience, whether objective or subjective. If we don't, we condemn ourselves to a limited model, because there are many things about which we have only incomplete knowledge. In other words, we have to act on a hypothesis (i.e., to some extent, on belief alone). Carl Jung said there is much in life that we can't yet understand, but that doesn't mean we have to pretend it doesn't exist.

Wisdom goes beyond that for which we have evidence. So accept the subjective—even the peculiar. Shakespeare has Hamlet say, "There are more things in heaven and earth, Horatio, than are dreamt of in your philosophy," and Wayne Dyer writes, "Let go of your conditioned way of needing proof in the physical world before something becomes your truth."

Starting points in practice

The key for a leader of people is to discern properly cause and effect—both tangible and intangible—and act accordingly. What part of an issue is your responsibility, and what part is someone else's? Answering these questions accurately takes much more work and presence of mind than we might imagine.

More often than we realise, we're creating the issue,

or at least failing to take the actions we could take to make things better. If the team isn't performing, yes, we might have the wrong people, but it's as likely that we haven't done everything we could do to stimulate a different outcome, perhaps by our own example. We are the most influential person present, after all. That's what a leader is, or should be.

History shows, time and again, that ordinary people are capable of extraordinary things, if led well.

Show up.

See clearly.

Sense your surroundings.

2

Leading and Following

Sustainable influence and the art of authority

With the greatest leader above them,
people barely know one exists.
— From the *Tao Te Ching*, 17th Verse

The chance to lead is elusive.

We need to understand the sources and legitimate uses of authority and what to do when none is formally vested in us. If we do have that kind of power through our employment or position, it is our duty to use it, and doing that effectively and appropriately is itself a challenge. Formal authority isn't always the asset it appears. Sometimes, it can be an inhibitor. It gets in the way and makes change harder to achieve because people fear authority. However, perhaps harder still is succeeding without formal authority, merely through trust and influence and natural leadership.

Even when we do have explicit authority, we'll achieve more sustainable results if we lead in a natural way rather than through diktat. Someone in a position of authority is likely to do a more sustainable job of leading and managing if they've had some experience of getting things done when they had no formal authority at all.

To put it another way, the issue is knowing how to succeed when we are not the boss. We will become better leaders if we draw on that experience when we are in charge. We need to see the distinction between personal power and positional power and to understand how to blend the two.

The problem with "pacing and leading"

So what's involved in leading without authority? How do we get into a position to have a leadership effect at all?

Before we can lead in any way, we must build a relationship with the people we hope may follow.

Coaching philosophies advocate a sensible-enough process of first following or "pacing" another person with the intent of establishing rapport. We should seek to make ourselves as much like the other as is reasonable. This is actually a natural human process—one we can make conscious and accelerate if we choose.

Once rapport is established, then we might seek to lead the other person towards an outcome, or along a path of change. Rapport needs to be maintained, and the person needs to be willing to move at some level if any of this is to be ethical and effective.

Rapport is rather all-or-nothing. Either it's there or it isn't in what's essentially an unconscious process. If we experience resistance in influencing another person in a particular direction, then we are better to stop trying and instead invest more time, attention, and energy in pacing the other person.

That's a valid approach.

However…

It's all very well one-to-one, but what about with larger numbers of people?

Should we follow or should we lead?

The trouble is…

If we're seeking to lead change on a larger scale, we need to be leading with some people, whilst simultaneously pacing others, and the difficulty is we can't tailor all of our communication to every person all of the time. Once you put something out there (like a book), it's out. You're leading, like it or not, and you have no opportunity at that point to tailor the message nor to do any more "following" within its pages.

Moreover…

If you're in business, for example, your customers and prospects might not like you leading them at all, though that depends on what business you're in. They might expect you to dance to their tune—to pace them in other words—and, if they're paying, they obviously have that prerogative.

Intending to influence organisations, you may spend all your time pacing and rarely get to the stage of leading. Unfortunately, you may end up helping maintain what you see as the *status quo*, achieving the very opposite of what you hope for and believe is required. Generally, there's a lot more money available to keep things the same than there is to change them. Inertia is usually better funded than progress.

So you might have to decide whether to break ranks and lead more emphatically.

On the other hand…

If you're thinking of change within an organisation you essentially control, if you just want to run a business better, it's perhaps a bit easier. Perhaps. Maybe you don't control it as much as you would ideally like. Maybe you still need to do a bit of following of your people to build the rapport you require to effect the change you want to see. John Kotter warns that: "It is enormously difficult to enact by sheer force the big changes often needed today to make organisations perform better."

Tribes are everywhere

To lead successfully, you need to understand "tribes."

We have a fundamental need to belong, as a hard-wired part of human nature. As Steven Pressfield says, "Fear of rejection isn't just psychological; it's biological. It's in our cells." Belonging comes at a very early stage in Maslow's hierarchy of needs. In pre-historic times, if we became separated from our group, we would be unlikely to survive, which means we have deep-seated behaviours around groups. The need to belong and avoid expulsion from the group is a powerful force. We tend to form tribes in organisations, in countries—everywhere, in fact. We think about "us and them," and if we use "we" to encompass both, we are still thinking of a tribe, albeit a bigger one. In organisations, tribes are, of course, synonymous with "silos"—otherwise known as departments, divisions, and directorates.

Typical tribal behaviours include being critical of what or who isn't in the tribe and defensive of who and what is in the tribe, often without much reason. If we are the leader of the tribe, we might want to think about these patterns of behaviour and whether they're helpful.

Professions are tribes, with well-established norms of behaviour.

The need to belong gives rise to one of the six "weapons of influence" described by Robert Cialdini (social proof, in this case), which has been exploited by some to exert a kind of leadership, not always for wholesome purposes. "Especially in an ambiguous situation, the tendency [is] for everyone to be looking to see what everyone else is doing," he writes. "We seem to assume that if a lot of people are doing the same thing, they must know something we don't. Especially when we are uncertain, we are willing to place an enormous amount of trust in the collective knowledge of the crowd." Frequently, of course, the crowd is mistaken because the people in it are themselves acting on the basis of (apparent) social proof. They're following the tribe. This is a very powerful effect with sometimes very serious consequences.

You can't stand out by fitting in

If you can't get noticed, you can't get heard.
If you can't get heard, you can't get the job done.

— Toni Newman

To lead on an issue, you need to get attention somehow, and to do that you need to stand out in some way. It's no use, therefore, trying to blend in, at least not all the time.

To lead, you need to accept the possibility of leaving the tribe and recognise that, as Steven Pressfield puts it, "the highest treason a crab can commit is to make a leap for the rim of the bucket."

Funnily enough…

Your coming to terms with that sentiment may be the very thing that causes the tribe to follow, as your courage and conviction draws attention and instils belief. Courage is compelling. It needs to be real acceptance, though; feigned won't do. You truly have to commit.

To succeed in leadership, you have to be not just better, but also different. You have to put yourself out there to be judged. As Wayne Dyer says, "Those who care least about approval seem to receive it the most."

We fear both significance and insignificance. To lead, we need to accept we are both significant and insignificant.

Wisdom is knowing I am nothing,
love is knowing I am everything,
and between the two my life moves.
— Nisaragadatta Maharaj

From nothing to something

Marketers talk about getting traction in the market, by which they mean achieving that point at which a business's actions start having a commercial effect. Well, it's very similar leading change. Actually, marketing is a form of leading change—change in a marketplace—and successful leadership involves a kind of marketing, so there are many useful parallels. At first, our wheels spin. We expend enormous energy, much more than we ever imagined, and nothing happens. Nothing. We are met with indifference, suspicion, and disbelief.

Eventually, somehow—and we're probably not quite sure how—somebody, somewhere gets it, and we begin to receive the feedback that allows us to refine what we're doing in such a way that gradually, more and more people take action.

But it usually takes a long time to get from nothing to something—much longer than we expect. So we must be patient and keep at it.

Connection and attention

If we trade in leadership…

Other people need to believe we have something different and better, so we need to show them what we have to offer. We need to show them our best ideas for free. If, like me, you were brought up always to safeguard intellectual property, this is a big shift.

If we're selling something tangible achieved by hidden means, we have the option of allowing interested parties to witness demonstrations or try the product, without revealing the secrets that make it possible.

But here's the thing…

With intangible know-how, it's different. Potential buyers will weigh the quality of the means as much as the results, so we need to show them what we've got to offer. Then, if they're impressed, they'll likely ask us to help them implement what they're learning from us.

So…

You need to put your ideas out there. You need to be prepared to be judged and to be comfortable at the centre of everyone's attention. You need people looking at you if you are going to lead change. If you don't have attention, you can't convey your message. This isn't necessarily easy: Some people are very uncomfortable being the focus of attention. Without that, though, leadership in general, and leadership of change specifically, will be difficult to achieve. The key to accepting everyone's attention is accepting yourself—which is part of the inner journey.

Personally...

It took me a while to come to terms with my version of this fear, but I realised that if I had some insights to share, I would have to make myself better known and draw attention, even though in truth I'd quite happily remain anonymous.

Status

Personal authority is tied up with "status"—relative interpersonal status. This is not the perceived status that attaches to a position in an organisation, for example, but the dynamic status that arises in a specific context, when we assess another person. You could call this "credibility" or "presence," too. For example, a speaker at an event has more status than an audience member, at least to begin with, provided they are properly introduced. How that speaker uses that relative status to put her message across is a key part of the art of public speaking, though not necessarily something she is aware of consciously.

So...

Just as in public speaking, in leadership, we need to acquire some relative status. However, a considerable difference in status may make our task harder rather than easier, because it may create a barrier between leader and follower. That's why a little self-deprecating behaviour, such as admitting a weakness, has its place.

So there's an art in cultivating some relative status, but no more than we need because that is liable to be counter-productive. Some study of the workings of theatre drama helps. That's where this perspective on status has its origins.

We need to match the force with which we impart our message of change to the level of relative status we hold. Get these out of kilter, and we won't achieve the effect we want. Too much force for our level of status and we'll be ignored; not enough force and we'll seem uncertain of our message. The tricky bit is, our relative status is different in different circumstances, depending on our audience at the time. So we need to adapt. We need to see who is "in front of us," as it were.

In learning from established leaders, we need to be aware of this factor. Those leaders may achieve a certain effect because they have the necessary status or presence. We can do exactly the same things they do and not achieve the same result because our status with our audience is different from their status with theirs. Our results depend on our "brand," and our brand is something our audience or our market determines, not us. We may seek to influence perception of our brand, but ultimately others decide. As Seth Godin says, "Being charismatic doesn't make you a leader. Being a leader makes you charismatic."

The handicap of authority

Positional power doesn't always help us. Formal authority is good for running an organisation in an unchanging, business-as-usual state and in certain short-term crises, but in times of evolution, formal authority can inhibit the social processes needed to develop truly emergent and grounded solutions.

Groups of people have power—much more than the power of any individual, however capable and experienced he or she may be. It's all too easy for workforces and teams accustomed to complying with authority to drop into that comfortable place of just doing what the leader says, but then the power of the group is lost.

On the other hand, sometimes you need a high level of coherence, and the easiest way to achieve that may be to form an organisation that places high importance on compliance and respect for authority.

So, if you are a holder of formal authority, you need to think about when it serves you and when it doesn't. Then you need to find ways of setting it aside when it's not helping.

Top-down and bottom-up

We're familiar with the hierarchical form of organisations, commonly represented with a triangle. Actually, the oldest form of organisation is the circle—

the village circle in which all present participate equally. One way of setting aside authority is convening in a circle. In making that choice, we're moving into the realm of "social capital" and the ability of communities of whatever kind to achieve things together without the presence of much or even any formal authority. This effect is particularly relevant to systems of participative (as opposed to representative) democracy, in which consumers resume their responsibilities as citizens. Choosing to draw on that effect is open to organisations everywhere.

In the words of Manfred Hellrigl, a specialist in social capital, the reality is every institution in the world depends on self-organising systems including families, companies, governments, hospitals, and countries. If the participants didn't take it upon themselves to make sure things worked, nothing would happen.

Hierarchy is needed too. Of course, it is. The problem arises when it becomes an end in itself. As the Hopper brothers, for example, point out in *The Puritan Gift*, decisions in organisations should be made as close to the "coal face" as possible.

A parallel example is the difference between traffic lights and a roundabout: Traffic lights are top-down control; a roundabout is a self-organising system. We do need to build the roundabout, though.

At the practical level, a number of specific approaches can be used to enable self-organisation. Just one example is the "Open Space Technology" approach to multi-party, and potentially large-scale, dialogue, which in its originator Harrison Owen's words, "works because self-organisation works," and enables diverse groups of all sizes to deal with complex and difficult issues in a very short period of time. For justification, he refers to "the growing consensus in the scientific community that the power of self-organisation underlies the emergence of the entire cosmos from the moment of the Big Bang until this present instant."

To lead or to follow?

For someone brought up to take charge of a situation and initiate the action required, I found it difficult to learn that leadership isn't always welcomed. For many years, I experienced a dilemma in ambiguous situations about whether to lead or whether to follow. My dilemma reflected an expectation of some degree of hierarchical structure, however transitory. Such is the power of conditioning.

Sometimes, my attempts to take on a leadership role would be rebuffed. Sometimes, my support for someone else leading would be ignored. For someone wanting to see things done, this was frustrating.

So I have struggled with this...

Whether to lead or to follow? If there is a middle way, what is it?

Quite recently, I realised that the reconciliation of leading and following is simply being present. As with many cases of blending "opposites," the answer isn't simply the midpoint on a spectrum; it's on another dimension altogether. So now I see that sometimes there is no need either to lead or to follow: It is enough to be present and available and connected.

You see...

Whose need are we seeking to fulfil by leading or following—the group's or ours? Ours, of course, and so we become entangled with the situation. So the lesson here is to detach from our need for the group—to be available if needed, but not to need to be needed.

What about you then?

How do you decide when to lead and when to follow? Are you able to be merely present, even as the boss? As Wayne Dyer says, "Allow rather than interfere... allowing is quite often the highest form of leadership."

The power of presence

Hold on! If we're merely present, how will we get anything done?

I struggled with this conundrum for a while. Just being present appears to imply being passive.

Eventually, I solved this dilemma by connecting it with something a number of sources say. For example, as Gene Early puts it, "It's not what you do that makes the difference, it's who you are when you do what you do." In other words, the nature and quality of your presence is the determining factor in what happens.

Some very effective ways of gathering people together in self-sustaining change work are available, but they all depend on the people leading the process being appropriately present and mindful of their own journey. As Bill O'Brien, former CEO of Hanover Insurance says, "The quality of the intervention is directly related with the inner state of the intervener." Paradoxically perhaps, large-scale systemic change can come down to doing small things well.

So most of our leadership effect (or not) is determined by our presence, mostly unconsciously. Looked at that way, choosing just to be present then makes complete sense—and ultimately is the way to get things done—because it is the way to establish the connection we need so that when we do act, others respond. In short, strong silence works.

> *Those who know do not talk.*
> *Those who talk do not know.*
>
> — From the *Tao Te Ching*, 56th Verse

The options available

If you have unequivocal authority to direct other people as a "manager" of some kind, for example, and if you use your power wisely, what you want to happen may well happen. On the other hand, if even a little ambiguity creeps in over who reports to whom and about what, your ability to get things done by mere instruction will rapidly diminish. At this point, you will need presence and, frankly, greater skill. For success in a role in which you have little or even no formal authority over the people whose contribution you need, such as that of a programme manager, you need the influence that comes with significant presence.

Once you're into the realm of leading change from business-as-usual in an organisation or influencing a community of people at large, the nature, strength, and integrity of your personal presence—including a willingness to follow as well as lead—are likely to be the critical factors, because, of course, whatever formal authority you may have had derives from the old order, not the new.

In any situation, understanding the nature and extent of your power, such as it may be, is the starting point.

To lead, be present, fully.

That may be all that is necessary.

3

Purpose and Resilience

Finding your inner strength

Success is the progressive realisation of a worthy goal.
— Earl Nightingale

Leading ourselves effectively includes developing a clear sense of purpose. We can approach that question at various levels, of course, but the deeper our contemplation, the more powerful the results. In the end, we must come to address the significance and meaning of our lives. Without some clarity in our individual answers to these profound questions, we are unlikely to conduct ourselves with any great power or personal authority or to lead other people effectively.

Seeing our purpose clearly is not the work of five minutes, though. Nor is it a task we ever completely finish. Our aim is ever-evolving through life, as is, for that matter, the vision we hold of how we would like things to be. Furthermore, we probably need to dovetail our vision and purpose with those of the people or organisations with whom we work.

A vision, with us in it

We detect rather than invent our missions in life.
— Victor Frankl

A vision is a description of a point in time. A purpose is a direction of travel towards a vision. Logically, one creates a vision before a purpose. However, the whole process of developing vision and purpose is iterative, so that's a bit of a pedantic distinction. Either way, having a vision is important, because it opens us up to noticing opportunities that will help us realise our desires.

Before we can create something in reality, we must create it in our heads. Our brains are primarily pattern-recognisers. Our unconscious mind draws our attention to sensory experience that matches in some way the thought structures we already have inside. So, if we want to notice those pieces passing by in the external world that relate to what we want, we need to set up the necessary internal patterns first. We do that by developing a vision.

You may well have had this experience: You're looking for a street but you can't remember its name. You drive about hoping to come across the place. Then you see a sign on the wall of a building and immediately recognise the name you're looking for but haven't been able to bring to mind. This happens because our neurology is much better at inputting than outputting.

A vision, then, is a future state of things that we hope to see made manifest—a dream, if you like. In articulating a vision, it helps the manifesting aspect if we describe our vision in the present tense, as if it's already happening. That sets up our unconscious to regard the vision as a real possibility now rather than some future state from which we are forever separated in time.

Now…

We need to include ourselves in our vision for it to be fully effective. If we create a vision of some improved external form of our organisation or the world at large, then sure, we'll recognise steps along the way when they happen in the external word—we'll be a well-informed spectator—but we won't be connected and involved, because we haven't set ourselves up to recognise parts of the pattern that have something to do with us.

Holding a vision that doesn't include ourselves is a mistake to which we are particularly prone if our vision is audacious. If we seek some change in the world we know is possible—change that we even can contribute to leading—one way of keeping ourselves safe, apparently, is not to write ourselves into the vision. Then we're not exposed. But the problem is that we won't recognise the opportunities that come our way to play our part. We haven't set up our internal patterns correctly. Instead, we've programmed ourselves to be an observer rather than an effective contributor. Active participation is liable to pass us by, as will remunerative reward for contributing.

On the bigger themes, we can be pretty sure other people will be working on the same issues, so our vision is at least gradually going to come into being whether we are involved or not. That's a good thing, of course, but if we want to be involved, we need to see ourselves in the game.

Creative tension

We might sometimes need to come to terms with the ambition of our vision and accept that it isn't going to happen immediately, however hard and effectively we work on it. It helps to perceive both our vision and our current reality, as well as the gap between the two. The art is to accept that the separation exists and be calm in the face of it, while at the same time, see that our purpose is to act to close the gap, however long it takes. Being clear about this gap between our current reality and our vision sets up a "creative tension," which we can both accept and be pulled forward by. Responding to that creative tension becomes our purpose.

If, to us, our vision is a compelling one—and if it isn't, why bother with it?—then our purpose will be strong and we will be energised—burning with a passion, even—to see the gap closed between how things are and how we would like them to be. The actual mode by which we progress is just a channel then. Acting as a manager, leader, director, coach, consultant, trainer, politician, public servant, entrepreneur, speaker, or some combination is a question of choice of medium.

The importance of an aim

A compelling vision gives us an aim.

Mark Beaumont, a long-distance cyclist, says that when he cycled round the world and broke the record of 276 days by 81 days, he in fact beat his target by eight hours. As he himself said, that seems to demonstrate the importance of having an aim or a goal.

Tolstoy's *War and Peace* draws out lessons of history from the French invasion of Russia in the Napoleonic period. When the French had the aim of reaching Moscow, their actions went pretty well. Once they got there, though, they no longer had a purpose, and the whole adventure fell apart with great loss of life. Tolstoy also makes clear that he thought Napoleon wasn't really leading. He was actually following. He was swept along by a popular desire to invade Russia. In other words, if we're "marching with the army," it's very difficult to change its direction. If we're going to lead, we'll need to find a way to do that, though.

Clarity of Purpose

When we have some clarity about how we would like things to be—our vision—we can work out what our specific purpose and role is in bringing that about.

Our vision, and so our purpose, flows ultimately from our values—what we see as important. We need to develop the detail of what we would actually like to see happen—what good looks like. How detailed does our vision need to be? Detailed enough that we "would recognise it if it showed up" as Peter Senge put it.

Sharing vision and purpose are also important in a collective context, an aspect to which we will return later.

Now…

It's up to us what our purpose turns out to be. It could quite simply be to earn money to provide for our family every month. That's perfectly reasonable. Alternatively, we may, for whatever reason, be driven to make a bigger impact than that and achieve some kind of change in the world. For example, Steve Jobs, co-founder of Apple Computers, wanted to "put a ding in the Universe," which he pretty much did, figuratively speaking at least.

Having a clear and compelling purpose is one important component of resilience.

He who has a why to live for can bear almost any how.

— Friedrich Nietzsche

Resilience—being your best self, consistently

Success requires us to step into and maintain powerful states of being—quickly, easily, and reliably. We can achieve this in a simple and effective way: by first developing our sense of the state we want and then thinking of a metaphorical representation of it.

Here's how this works…

Be in a calm place and think of yourself at your best in the type of situation you want to focus on—a state you would like to access whenever you want. Think of handling whatever it is you want to handle effortlessly, successfully, and easily. Either recall a time when you were exactly as you want to be or imagine being that way now. Notice what you see, what you hear, and what you feel like. Notice where in your body you experience the sensation of that feeling, and what the sensation is—for example, it might be a feeling of relaxation or perhaps a tingling. Whatever it is for you is right.

Now…

Find a powerful metaphor for the state by asking yourself: "And that's like what?" What is a symbolic representation for you in your ideal state? Go with what comes into your head, however odd it seems. It's just for you, after all. Metaphors can be weird. You see, our unconscious knows what we need, but it plays by different rules from our linear, conscious, thinking brain. As you notice what the metaphor could be—the imaginary representation of that resourceful state of being—amplify it to make it as powerful as possible. Make it a supreme example in terms of size, appearance, colour, sound, feel, or whatever is important to you. When you've got that, notice how the epitomised version strengthens your state of being in real-world terms. When you recall your metaphor, the power comes back. Use the metaphor to access that state whenever you want. Thinking of it will take you into the posture, the manner, the detailed behaviours, and so on that you need.

Some examples will help make this real…

A successful business owner had difficulty believing in herself. With coaching, she recalled a situation in which she felt she was doing a great job and really "in the zone." When asked, "And that's like what?"—she said, "A toaster." She described an especially well-made and pleasing toaster, but nevertheless, a toaster. Just recalling the toaster was enough for her to go back to doing a great job and being "in the zone." All the associated posture and beliefs and behaviours came back, triggered by that one word, "toaster." If the resourceful metaphor seems surprising to you, bizarre even, that's a sign it has come from the right place—your unconscious. You didn't think your way to it, and it's adding something.

For a friend who hosts events and wants to fill the room with a warm, welcoming energy, the metaphor is "sunshine." Another is "lighter than air" when speaking in public. A third is "snow-boarding," embodying a sense of relaxed control, again as a speaker.

Another young man wanted "things not to get to him so much." Now here's a very important point: His original desired state, had a "not" in it. We needed to turn it round, to "say it the way he wanted it." We agreed that we could say it as "things just bounce off" him. His metaphor for that turned out to be a steel ball.

Once you have your metaphor, say to yourself "I am a…" (whatever your metaphor is) and notice how it brings back the state you want, which you can then refine and strengthen. Practice this enough so it is available to you when you need it.

This little process is enough to change your life. It works very well because the metaphor taps into the power of your unconscious, and it has the same structure as the real world effect you want. They're "isomorphic" with each other. It's that similarity at the deeper level that matters and is useful. We could say the metaphor is a model of the state you want. Just bringing the symbolic representation to mind recalls all the attributes embodied in the model when you need them. The beauty of it is, you only need to remember one word or a short phrase to access a powerful version of yourself when you need to be at your best.

Here we're drawing on the underused area of symbolic modelling and the associated questioning skills (called "Clean Language") that can be used to great effect to work with unconscious representations of our lives and our issues.

Keep the rubbish out

You become what you think about.

— Earl Nightingale

We attract more of what we are, and what we are is determined by what's in our heads (i.e., what we're thinking about).

So…

Be really careful what you let into your mind—your "head space." If you watch television or listen to radio, you risk letting the predominant mood of the station set your own. For example, if you hear a lot of aggressive questioning, that's what you're going to attract into your own life. Your day is going to be filled with aggressive questioning. Do not delegate control of your head space to some faceless producer or editor. Keep that for you alone.

If you want to be a great leader of yourself or anyone else, get the rubbish out of your head and keep it out. That'll help you be resilient in the face of setbacks.

Filling your head with inconsequential thoughts—in other words, noise—isn't the same as being peaceful. Similarly, filling your body with the literal rubbish of a poor diet or nicotine, alcohol, or caffeine to become numb isn't the same as being peaceful, either.

That said, please understand...

I too enjoy a glass of something, but I know it's not a way to be peaceful—anaesthetised, perhaps, but not peaceful. Numbing out is not the same as chilling out. We are the finely tuned results of billions of years of evolution. The closer we can keep to the chemistry we are optimised for, the better we'll do.

Build your calmness

The still is the master of unrest.

— From the *Tao Te Ching*, 26th Verse

The calmer we are, the more ability we have to choose our response to what happens to us and so the more control we have over the outcome. It's no use thinking of this at the last minute, though. Calmness needs to be part of our being. The best way to achieve this is with a simple meditative practice.

Here's one…

Sit in a quiet place without distractions in an upright, comfortable position with your feet flat on the floor and your hands at rest on your thighs. Place your gaze on a point in front of you a little above eye level—something specific to focus on, like a mark on a wall. You'll also need some way of knowing how much time has passed. Glancing at a clock or a watch will do.

Sit for 20 minutes, looking at your chosen spot and paying attention to your breathing, in and out. Keep your eyes open to stay awake.

The aim is not to think about anything, to quiet your mind. However, thoughts will come into your head, of course. Instead of developing them and feeding them energy, notice each one and let it pass without reacting to it. Typically, some time will go by without you thinking of anything, and your awareness will only be on your breathing. Then you will realise you are thinking about something and that the thought is growing. Instead of pushing the thought away harshly, though, let go of it gently and calmly, and return your awareness to your breathing. You will probably go through this cycle many times, possibly more often at the beginning than at the end of your 20 minutes.

You may find that the thoughts are insistent, demanding your attention and energy because of their seeming importance. The benefit of meditation comes from learning to acknowledge them and let them go, without feeding them. As you do this, the thoughts gradually come less frequently and insistently. We could probably find a biochemical explanation for this: As we stop reinforcing the urgency of our thoughts, changing hormonal levels in our brain slow down its generation of new appeals for our attention, and the thoughts seem less insistent.

The thing is…

There is only the present moment. That's all there ever is. Very little truly won't wait in the present moment, unless the building is on fire or something. Buddhist philosophy would say there is no past and no future; no judgment and no grasping (or pushing away).

You may find that 20 minutes goes by surprisingly quickly—more quickly than 20 minutes waiting for a train, for example. (Waiting for a train or anything else, by the way, is a good opportunity to meditate.)

When the time is up, move on to whatever you intended to do next. Make good use of the calm state you've created for yourself. You will find that you can focus well. In addition, you will have strengthened your resources of calmness for dealing with whatever happens in the course of your day.

Here's a parallel…

The guidelines for online forums often say something like "Don't feed the trolls," meaning don't respond to abusive participants because they're just looking for an argument. Meditation (and life, actually) is a bit like that: Don't feed the thoughts you don't want. Learn not to respond to the people who "push your buttons." They will lose interest and go somewhere else.

Another physical approach to calmness is learning the habit of being in "peripheral vision," which produces parasympathetic nervous arousal—the opposite of a "fight, flight, or freeze" response. The technique is set out in *Relationship Mastery*, and you can find it online.

Eckhart Tolle writes: "The mind is a superb instrument if used rightly. Used wrongly, however, it becomes very destructive. To put it more accurately, it is not so much that you use your mind wrongly—you usually don't use it at all. It uses *you*. This is the disease. You believe you are your mind" (as Descartes unhelpfully declared). "This is the delusion. The instrument has taken you over." Instead, "The moment you start *watching the thinker*, a higher level of consciousness becomes activated."

The Bhagavad Gita, which is a classic of Indian spirituality from somewhere between the fifth and second centuries BC, speaks of understanding "the difference between the field and the Self, the knower," as Diana Morrison explains. "Most people confuse the two, taking the body and mind to be who they are. We may be totally unaware that there is a Self, a consciousness underneath the surface awareness of a separate 'I.'" In fact, both body and mind are aspects of the field. The mind is not the knower. The knower is the Self, and it watches the mind.

The best way to experience this crucially important point in a very practical way is to sit quietly for a moment and become fully aware that in the gap between your thoughts, the presence that remains and observes your thoughts coming and going is the real, unchanging you—your Self. Identifying with that presence rather than your mind will change your life in all sorts of liberating ways. This is the exact opposite of what our education and our culture tend to condition us to do—to identify ourselves with our mind and our ego (which, some say, stands for "earth guide only" or "edging God out").

Diana Morrison adds: "Just as physics no longer regards matter and energy as essentially separate, *The Gita* would not regard matter and mind as separate; they are different aspects of the underlying 'stuff' of existence"—the field. Our calling is to be consciously the knower—the Self—and disentangled from the field.

Resilience

People frequently ask me, "Where should I look for strength?" One client remarked, for example, that he always seemed to need a father figure, clearly thinking of external role models or sources of inspiration. Ultimately, though, these are all transient for one reason or another. Searching around outside is looking in the wrong place. The only dependable answer is inside.

So…

Find your spirit—your inner "father figure." Something I found very helpful was a line Marianne Williamson quotes from a spiritual text called *A Course in Miracles*. It says, "If you don't lean on me, you will lean on other people." "Me" in that sentence means spirit or God, whatever that means to you. The more we do things which are "out there" with no map (i.e., the more we lead), the more we need to be in touch with our inner life force—our soul, some would say.

The Bhagavad Gita has a similar sentiment: "Abandon all supports and look to me for protection. I shall purify you from the sins of the past; do not grieve." As in *A Course in Miracles*, the statement is expressed in the voice of an inner spirit. As Eknath Easwaran writes about *The Gita*, "The words mean simply to cast aside external props and dependencies and rely on the Self alone, seeking strength nowhere but within."

I know this is deep stuff, but it's very important. It's what we've conditioned ourselves to avoid, especially in organisations…

Let me say how it is for me… If there's a God, it's inside. It's an inner thing—something immanent (there's that word I drew your attention to)—a spirit energy present everywhere, including in you and in me. So what will keep us on track despite all the buffeting of life is being in touch with that inner knowing that we're doing what we're meant to be doing—living on purpose, if you like.

I actually don't know any other way than this to bring about the permanent change in resilience most of us seek. We need some kind of spiritual answer—not necessarily a religious one, though it could be.

Basically, you need a faith in something—the energy of the Universe or whatever. Then you lean on that—inside. Having learned to do that, I've felt physically different ever since because my awareness of strength is much more internal than before. That resilience is entirely open to you too.

Eckhart Tolle's view on the difference between spirituality and religion helps: "In essence," he says, "there is and always has been only one spiritual teaching, although it comes in many forms. Some of these forms, such as the ancient religions, have become so overlaid with extraneous matter that their spiritual essence has become almost completely obscured by it."

In the end, we must find our strength within, rather than from other people, though they may perhaps help. Being our own source of belief is not such an easy thing to step into. All manner of influences in our environment—some of them very powerful—would like us to be dependent on them. They are best ignored.

Faith and belief

You never change things by fighting existing reality.
To change something, build a new model that makes the existing model obsolete.

— Buckminster Fuller

If you're working with a team and you are the leader,

where is belief in its success going to come from? The answer, of course, can only be you. Seth Godin writes: "Faith is the unstated component in the work of a leader, and I think faith is underrated. Paradoxically, religion is vastly overrated."

Sometimes we're not sure whether to believe something or not. In many cases, the evidence is lacking. So we may as well choose the belief that may help us succeed, rather than its opposite.

Some time ago, I taught my youngest son to set the table—easy for most, but not for him because he has Autism. It took three months, and at the beginning the task looked impossible. I thought, "I'm never going to manage this," but I persevered, choosing to believe it was possible, breaking the task down into small steps, and keeping going even when all the feedback told me it wasn't going to be possible. Eventually, he could do it.

So now I ask myself…

What else could I do if I choose to believe it's possible, break it down into small enough steps, and keep going even when all the evidence tells me it isn't possible?

Many things are like this. There is a kind of threshold we have to reach before results flow at all. In a new business, for example, or a change programme, we have to maintain our rising line of increasing effort, skill, and profile before we succeed in achieving something new with any consistency. Before we reach that threshold, it can seem as if nothing is working. The only thing that can sustain us is belief. There isn't any evidence. Faith alone, therefore, may determine the outcome.

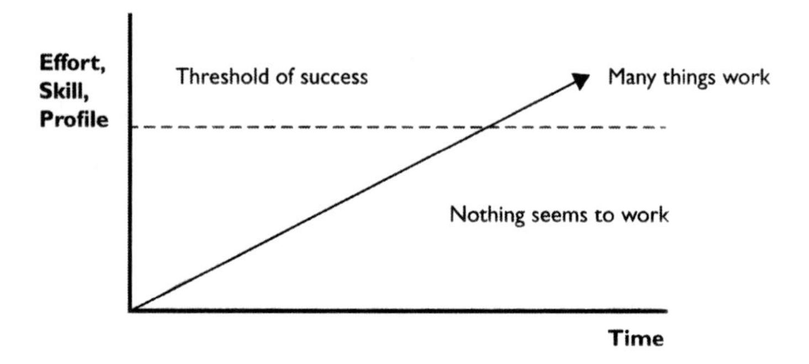

Now…

What could you do if you choose to believe it's possible, break it down into small enough steps, and keep going even when all the evidence tells you it isn't possible?

Trust in belief: Often, that's all that truly separates success and failure. After all, what is the definition of "impossible?" Really, only that something hasn't happened yet. As Dee Hock says, "Possibility cannot be determined by opinion, only by attempt."

In leadership, belief comes before evidence.

4

Your Unconscious Companion

The one you really need to influence

Every extension of knowledge arises from making conscious the unconscious.

— Friedrich Nietzsche

Before we can be effective leaders and especially masters of transformational change, in ourselves or in others, we need to become well versed in the ways of the unconscious mind. Among other things, we need an acute awareness of the difference between conscious and unconscious behaviour, as well as a close relationship with our own inner being.

Most of our behaviour arises from patterns formed long ago in our lives and repeats itself almost of its own volition. It's clearly not literally true to say that our unconscious mind is a different person with whom we must build a relationship, but it's quite helpful to think of it that way. We need to get to know that presence, to befriend the creature within. Putting it like that is almost literally correct because our unconscious behaviour stems from those parts of our brain—the limbic system—that are more primitive in evolutionary terms than the neo-cortex where our conscious thought arises. It really is like we have an animal inside—and a very powerful and intelligent one at that.

In fact…

The great majority of what we do is determined by our unconscious mind, and so all lasting change comes about through a shift in our unconscious programming—our habits, if you like.

As we become aware of the unconscious in ourselves and are better able to influence it, so we will see its presence in other people, usually much more clearly than they see it in themselves, if they see it at all. This matters because actual leading and following—the real effect, that is—is a largely unconscious process.

Leadership involves fascination, and as Sally Hogshead writes: "Most elements of fascination work at the subconscious level... We are, if only for a moment, utterly spellbound" because "fascination strips away our usual rational barriers." Not so surprisingly, she found in her research, "The majority of people don't find their bosses even mildly fascinating."

Seeing what's really going on

What you don't realise is most of your life is unconsciously determined.

— Milton Erickson

Our unconscious mind runs our life, mostly. The majority of what we do, we do without thinking. For example, if you drive a car or operate some other complex machinery or device, how aware are you of all the detailed actions you need to take to achieve the result you desire? The answer, of course, is you are not very aware of them at all.

We can travel from home to work, for instance, without being conscious of the journey itself. We can easily devote our thinking to our plans for the day, while our unconscious faculties take care of all the complex details of keeping our body functioning, operating the mechanics of our car, and making our way through the traffic, all at the same time. Only when we're going somewhere unfamiliar, do we need to become conscious of the journey.

Much of what happens in our lives is taken care of in a similar fashion. Our ability to do repetitive activities without conscious thought is a great asset, but it can also trap us in old ways of being and doing that don't work so well any more. Just because we enact a habit successfully doesn't mean it's useful or the best choice. In presenting Carl Jung's thinking, Ruth Snowden writes: "The unconscious is always in danger of becoming too one-sided, keeping to well-worn paths and getting stuck in dead ends."

So we need to become aware of our unconscious patterns of behaviour and learn how to change them. That may sound difficult, but it's not so hard: Our unconscious mind is a bit like a pet—a dog, for example—that we can train with simple instructions and repetition, which is, after all, how we learned to drive.

Your conscious mind isn't in full control

Here's a simple practical demonstration: Stand on one leg, with that knee slightly bent to help you balance. With your other foot off the ground, move it in a clockwise, circular fashion. Once you have established that pattern, try drawing the figure six in front of you using the hand on the same side of your body as the circling foot and notice what happens. Most people find that their foot starts moving the same way that they're drawing the six—counter-clockwise—because when we attempt the exercise, our unconscious mind gets involved.

Here's what's happening…

Our limbic brain—our animal brain, if you like—is intervening and saying, "Oh no, you don't," because our survival as an animal is rather closely tied up with what we do with our body. Our unconscious mind won't let us do things, especially with our feet, that appear to put us at risk, and so it keeps tight control. (If we use the hand on the opposite side from the foot to draw the six, incidentally, the job is easier, with less interference between the two tasks and less apparent risk.)

This is a physical parallel of the mental "resistance," articulated by Steven Pressfield, which tries to keep us psychologically safe, but which may inadvertently hold us back from success. Our unconscious mind tends to keep us in our comfort zone.

It can seem like our unconscious mind inhabits not just our brain, but also our whole body. In the foot-circling exercise, the powerful presence that intervenes and stops us doing the opposing rotations seems to arise in our limbs as much as in our mind. In the Western world especially, we've been conditioned to believe that our intelligence resides exclusively in our head, but that really isn't the case. Intelligence and power is distributed all over our body, giving rise to the phrase "muscle memory."

Could you train yourself to turn your hand one way and your foot the other? Probably. You really can train your unconscious, which is what you do in learning to play a musical instrument by much repetition of gradually more complicated movements.

Carl Jung found it significant that in many cultures he had visited, most notably India, "people still lived in the whole body and had not retreated to live only from the head, as they had in the West," so they had remained more physically and mentally integrated and thus better connected with their unconscious mind.

Try the foot-circling exercise when you can. It's very important you experience for yourself how powerful and "involuntary" the effect is. That's the force we need to get to know and collaborate with.

The role of the unconscious mind

The unconscious mind stores and organises memories and makes associations. It runs and preserves the body, manages energy, and is the domain of the emotions. The unconscious mind forms perceptions and transmits them to the conscious mind. It suppresses or presents emotions, as the case may be, to protect us, or seek our conscious attention, sometimes at inconvenient times.

Logical reasoning and analysis, and more complex forms of communication, on the other hand, are functions of the conscious mind.

The unconscious mind works symbolically rather than with language. It maintains instincts and gains habits through repetition. We can train it with practice (or ritual, which is how indoctrination works). We can also influence the unconscious with storytelling, because that mode of communication tends to bypass the conscious mind. We can access the unconscious with hypnosis, which achieves a similar effect more directly with the cooperation of the person involved.

The unconscious will do a good job of delivering results if given clear direction. It continually seeks gain and will always take the path of least resistance, like an animal. So if we increase another person's options or awareness of their options, we can safely assume they will make the best choice—according to their criteria, though, not ours.

The unconscious doesn't process negatives. It can't tell the difference between "stressed" and "not stressed," for example. It just knows what stress is.

Now…

If you think the unconscious mind does sound a bit

like an animal, that's not surprising, because that's what it is, more or less. It responds to its environment, often with remarkable power, like a tiger.

The unconscious takes it personally

Your unconscious mind takes everything personally because it doesn't have a sense of separateness. It's unable to distinguish between itself and others. It can't tell the difference between something said of someone else and something said of you (and that applies to everyone else, of course). So if you're angry with someone else or about someone else, your unconscious thinks you're annoyed with yourself and it gets upset accordingly. (Imagine a sad-looking dog inside.)

Furthermore, if you express anger about a third party to someone you are talking to, that person's unconscious can't tell the difference between you being angry with the third party and you being angry with her. Exactly the same applies with favourable emotions too, so if you express warmth towards a person, everyone else present feels it too. That can be useful.

The scientific explanation for this is in the area of "mirror neurons," which have been shown to activate when we see someone else experiencing something we identify with.

So be careful what you say, and to whom. They'll take it personally even if it's not literally about them. Your own inner being will, too.

Our unconscious mastery

Most of our leadership effect is unconscious, partly because the things we do best are our unconscious competences. In a sequence that will be familiar, we go from not knowing that we don't know how to do something, to knowing that we don't know, to knowing how to do it, and finally to doing it "without thinking," like this…

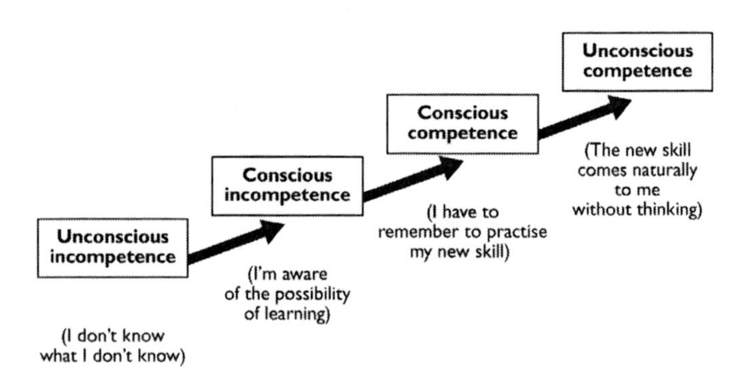

That much is probably familiar.

What may not be so plain is that the things we are best at, we do unconsciously. So, not only do we not really know how we do what we do well, we don't know what those things are. Ask someone what she thinks you do best, and you may well be surprised at her answer, because she'll be talking about your unconscious expertise.

Unconscious competences are also the reason why highly skilled people have difficulty describing how they do what they do. The reality is, they don't really know. With the best of intentions, they will attempt to explain the processes they use, but something will be missing. They'll unwittingly omit critically important, unconscious components of their art, and without these, we won't be able to recreate their results. We need to replicate all the elements of an expert's practice, including the unconscious ones, such as body language, facial expressions, tone of voice, physical environment, and so on—not just the cerebral part—to succeed.

Unconscious following and learning

"If you're in a room with people, you just get their stuff," says Derek Arden, a professional speaker, meaning we learn from them automatically. That's because a lot of our learning happens unconsciously, so it doesn't much matter if we're just one of many hundreds present. We actually don't even need to pay all that much deliberate attention to the process of assimilation. In fact, it would be quite hard to prevent it from occurring. (So be careful whom you associate with.)

This happens in organisations too. They're populated mostly by people behaving and learning unconsciously. Most of what they do, they do without thinking.

As a leader, you need to make sure your unconscious behaviour is consistent with your conscious intentions—what you want people to copy—because it's mostly your unconscious behaviour they will pick up (and, moreover, they'll do that unconsciously). That's why it's so important to do a good job of leading yourself if you hope to lead other people—so that your unconscious model is as you intend—and, once again, why you need to go first. As John Kotter says, "Nothing undermines change more than behaviour by important individuals that is inconsistent with the verbal communication"—in other words, leaders unconsciously doing the opposite of what they are espousing.

Who's setting your aspirations?

"The rat race is for rats. We're not rats; we're human beings." So said Jimmy Reid, who, it would be fair to say, is remembered in Scotland as a man of the people, and a rather left-wing one at that. He was centrally involved in a piece of socialist history: the sit-in at Upper Clyde Shipbuilders in 1971. Shortly after, he was elected Rector of Glasgow University and in his inaugural address, somehow captured the mood of the time with some eternal truths delivered in his compelling style. Remarkably, his words made front-page news around the world.

Among other things, he said that in many organisations, the greatest resource was the untapped potential of its people. And that, of course, is true. One of the most important tasks of a leader is to bring out that untapped potential.

We can start closer to home though…

Our greatest resource is the untapped potential in ourselves, and our first task begins there.

So what is waiting to be unlocked within you? Might you be a shadow of your future self?

You are. We all are.

So think about who you will be at some future time. The stereotypical interviewer's question—"Where do you want to be in three years' time?"—addresses a different thing. It's really about what you're going to be doing. Instead, look inward at who you are and who you are becoming, not what you're doing. There's a big difference.

So who are you going to be?

And what are you waiting for?

If you can describe a future version of yourself that appeals, why wait? If you're holding back, it's most likely because you're waiting to feel safe, but the thing is, no one else is going to come along and say: "I invite you to become your future self." In fact, some people might rather you didn't, for one reason or another.

Next time you're in company, take a look around and notice all the untapped potential in other people.

Here's the thing…

If they chose to look, they'd see it in you too.

As Seth Godin says, "Don't wait to be picked. Pick yourself." In Leo Tolstoy's *The Death of Ivan Ilyitch*, Ivan Ilyitch is a government official who essentially lived for himself. He falls mysteriously ill, and it becomes apparent he is dying. His learning comes right at the end, too late to make a difference. He looks at his wife and says, "What if my whole life has been wrong?" So, as Wayne Dyer put it, "Don't die with your music still in you."

A senior and wealthy industrialist, on being presented with a lifetime achievement award, said in his acceptance speech he now realised that he and his generation could have done more about environmental issues and global poverty, but they never chose to. This man does a great deal of charitable work, to be fair, but still it was clear he regretted not doing more.

In the end, of course, it's about getting in touch with our inner purpose—what we sense we are really here to do—connecting with our spirit, in fact, and sticking with something because we know it's right. That's what makes people inspirational—being "in spirit." The literal meaning of the word is a clue.

If we're truly leading, we're making our own map. If there is already a map for what we're doing, we're actually following. So if we want to lead, we need to get used to not having a map to follow. That can be lonely. So we need a kind of faith.

Are you following your parents' map?

It's remarkable how much control our parents have over us, including ones who aren't around any more, even if they never intended that. We're usually still unconsciously following their map, at least in part. Quite senior people can still be rather noticeably their parents' children. To be a great leader, you need to shift this. Have a good hard look at who you are being because you think your parents wanted you to be that way. Chances are they actually didn't. Mine have been gone a long time, so I've had a while to work this through and come to a kind of clarity about it.

It could be you feel at some level you don't want to outdo your parents...

We can deal with this one quite easily: If you are a parent yourself—and please imagine it if you're not—chances are you would be very happy for your children to do better than you, would you not? Here's the thing: You can be pretty sure your parents had the same hopes for you.

Actually, it's probably even simpler...

Your parents' continuing desire, whether they are around or not, and whether they say it or not, is probably just for you to be happy.

So set yourself free.

Learned limitations

As well as having limitations that stem from our upbringing, either because they were imposed on us or because of how we interpreted our experiences, we also learn limitations in later life.

Apparently, if you put fleas in a jar and cover it with a plate, the fleas will learn not to jump so high that they hit the lid. Then, if you take the plate away, the fleas can no longer jump out of the jar. They have learned a limitation. Speaking to an audience of managers and executives of an industrial plant, I was struck by how the very controlling corporate management culture had taught these people limitations that inhibited their ability to see viable futures for themselves outside the company, even when they had the chance to leave on generous terms. They were thoughtful when I provided several examples of very active people 20 years their senior. More prominently, Winston Churchill became Prime Minister of Britain—for the first time—at age 65.

Sometimes respected friends and peers say they're surprised to see us doing what we're doing. They mean well usually, though they're effectively saying we no longer fit within the limits they unconsciously perceive for us.

Be free of limitations.

Counter-intuitive or counter-habit?

When it comes to learning, we often say something is "counter-intuitive" as if "intuitive" is some kind of absolute, but of course it isn't. It might be part of common learning from shared experience—part of what Carl Jung called the "collective unconscious"—but it's still something learned. Some use the word "intuitive" to indicate that the source could be spirit in some form. They refer to "intuitive writing," for example, meaning that they channel something beyond themselves. Here, by "intuitive," I mean simply learning that arises from previous experience and is held or generated unconsciously.

So when we say something is "counter-intuitive," what we're actually saying is it runs counter to the learning or programming in our unconscious mind. It's "counter-habit," in other words.

Something that appears counter-intuitive to one person is accepted knowledge to another. It depends on your worldview. Learning something "counter-intuitive" is just an update to your or another's map of the world. No more than that.

Similarly, what some people dismiss as "theory" is knowledge that doesn't seem to fit with their unconscious programming. It's not their practice. Their own practice wouldn't seem like theory to them, you see.

Dual control

We could delve more deeply into the neuroscience of what functions arise in which part of our brain and nervous system, but it's not important for our purposes here. What is important to know is that much of our behaviour arises unconsciously, so to lead effectively, we need both to be aware of that and also to be able to influence unconscious programming through various means—primarily effective relationships and repeated communication.

There is a cyclic structure to this: First, conscious control and repetition progressively leads to changes in our unconscious patterning. Second, and completing the circle, unconscious patterning determines our day-to-day behaviour and our feelings, which influence our conscious thought.

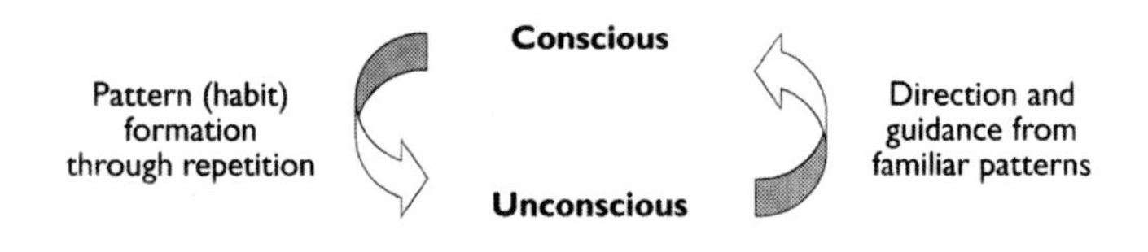

This circle has a "chicken and egg" character—which came first? Well, both. However, we can intervene in the cycle, and if we do so with enough consistency, we can utterly transform ourselves, as we can others, if that is what they want. When somebody says such and such behaviour is "just the way I am," she's really saying those are the actions that fit with her unconscious programming. Her unconscious is complaining: "This isn't what I'm used to!"

Ultimately, everything is a choice. It may not seem like it, but it is. That's why if we can keep ourselves off an unhealthy food option for a month or so, we may find we don't want it any more. Changed patterns after a time become the new reality—"the new me," as we might say.

As Will Durant wrote, summarising Aristotle: "Excellence is an art won by training and habituation: we do not act rightly because we have virtue or excellence, but we rather have these because we have acted rightly; we are what we repeatedly do. Excellence, then, is not an act but a habit."

All the time, we're training the animal inside, which is our unconscious, whether we're aware of it or not, so we might as well be deliberate about it.

The unconscious in leadership

The most important processes that bind a team together are unconscious ones. Indeed, what we call culture in organisations or society at large is the sum of unconscious behaviours. That's why it's often hard to change. We need to begin by making people aware of what they are unconsciously doing; we need to bring their habits to their attention.

Where many go wrong in leadership is acting as if conscious thought is enough, and that leading and following is a largely cerebral activity. It isn't. That's why so much communication about change is required—to achieve the repetition the unconscious requires. Then it will consistently deliver the results we hope to see.

When we communicate with people, we'd like to think it's the thinking, conscious brain that's listening. In fact, it's the creature inside—the limbic brain—that makes the first assessment about whether what we're saying merits conscious thought or not. Balancing comfort and tension is the way to keep people engaged—not too safe, not too dangerous. Alert but not fearful is the effect we want. In leading a team, we can share the uncertainties and challenges with them. They can handle it. In fact, it keeps them on board.

Work with the unconscious.

It's almost entirely responsible

for what happens.

5

Knowing and Not Knowing

Appropriate certainty, healthy doubt

Forget your perfect offering
There is a crack in everything
That's how the light gets in.

— Leonard Cohen

Doubt is healthy; conviction is necessary. We need to be open to learning, and yet we need to act.

Sensing when we know and when we don't know is a key skill—not an area where we can have perfect acuity, but still a vital sense for the leader to develop as much as possible. Sometimes, we need the "certainty" of knowing in order to act effectively and to lead. Other times, we're better to adopt an attitude of not knowing in order to be open to new possibility, to be curious. There's very little point to being active and wrong, after all.

The thing is…

We don't really know how our world works. Perhaps collectively, we come close, but individually, we're a long way off. We don't have the necessary breadth of knowledge. Moreover, our everyday experience suggests an understanding of things that is often at odds with what science knows at a deeper level. In general, things may not be what they seem. We may think we know, but we don't really. As Karl Popper said, "Knowledge is a sophisticated statement of ignorance."

At the same time, if we truly have knowledge in a situation, we need to take action based on that knowledge, such as it is. That can be hard. In some cultures, we are expected to "play small," to deny our own power, and to pretend we don't know when actually we do.

We seem to have a paradox—well, not so much a paradox as a constant need to be weighing and testing the validity of our knowledge, so that we can make the right decisions about whether to act, and if so, in what way.

Getting this balance right is vital: We need to recognise we know something useful when truly we do, and accept that we don't when probably we don't. We need a sense of timing too: If it's the right moment for action, we may need to "go with what we've got."

When it comes time to act, you have to oversimplify.

— Frank Farrelly

All is not what it seems: Part 1—Just empty space

Hard materials like steel or diamond or even wood seem solid, both to our touch and to our eye, but of course, we know they aren't. A modest knowledge of atomic structure tells us these substances are made up of atoms that are mostly empty space. So the materials we experience as solid are actually anything but. Our senses deceive us. The world isn't made up the way it appears at all.

Take the very simplest atom, Hydrogen: If the single

proton in its nucleus were the size of a tennis ball, the single electron orbiting that nucleus would be a speck of dust about a mile away. So the volume is made up almost exclusively of empty space. More complex atoms are like this too, and so, therefore, are we—mostly empty space. Yet we think of ourselves as solid.

At school, we were taught about protons, neutrons, and electrons, but not about the other more exotic subatomic particles nuclear physicists know exist. Take neutrinos, for instance: Very tiny subatomic particles that interact only very weakly with their environment, they pass through normal matter unimpeded, including right through the Earth, for example. In fact, about 65 billion neutrinos emanating from the Sun pass through every square centimetre of you, me, and the Earth every second. Are you aware of them?

I didn't think so.

How easy is it to believe neutrinos really do that?

We hold beliefs taught to us at a younger age more tightly than beliefs we come across in later life, like this outlandish-seeming tale about neutrinos. We're pretty happy to accept the existence of protons, electrons, and neutrons because we learned about them in our impressionable years, whereas neutrinos, positrons, mesons, bosons, and the rest seem almost like the stuff of science fiction.

Here's the thing…

What other beliefs that you learned at a young age do you hold tight and which might now be wrong? And what beliefs do you resist because they only came along later, but which might be right?

Human beings perhaps aren't really intended to change their knowledge in adult life—as a weakness of neurological design, I mean—but maybe they need to.

All is not what it seems: Part 2—Duality

Matter consists ultimately of subatomic particles in lots of empty space, but even those particles might not be solid. In certain circumstances, they can seem to behave more like waves of energy. The specific features of quantum physics are a consequence of this wave-particle duality. With the right apparatus, protons and electrons, for example, can be observed behaving sometimes like waves and sometimes like particles, depending on the circumstances. In fact, this duality is thought to be true of all matter; it's just that larger masses moving at much slower speeds correspond to much shorter wavelengths, way below our ability to observe.

Because of their wavelike properties, electrons that are constrained to exist in a confined space—such as that surrounding the nucleus of an atom—can only occupy certain discrete energy levels. That's because their wave nature means only certain frequencies and their multiples fit the space in which standing wave patterns are feasible, much like a violin or guitar string, thus producing a stable atom. Those allowed frequencies correspond directly to discrete "quantised" energy values.

All sorts of important macro-scale properties arise

from these restrictions in subatomic energy levels. Our world depends on them in many different ways: some of them entirely natural, others man-made.

Are electrons really waves or particles?

The answer, of course, is they are neither. They're something else that we can't perceive and have no words for. We experience that something else as either a wave or a particle depending on the circumstances, but it isn't actually either of these things, which are merely the alternative forms of our incomplete perception.

All is not what it seems: Part 3—Relativity

Everything is relative. There is no absolute or "preferred" frame of reference.

We know strange things happen when objects travel at speeds approaching the speed of light. Albert Einstein showed us in his Special Theory of Relativity that in these circumstances, the only way physics makes sense is if the passage of time isn't a constant everywhere. Rather, the speed of light is constant. To make sense of what happens when an object travels very fast, we have to abandon the constraint of time being a constant and accept that it slows down for objects travelling close to the speed of light, and moreover, that their length contracts too.

Now even that hard-to-grasp reality is only a special case—one that applies when frames of reference move at constant speed. Allow gravity and acceleration fully into the picture, and we come to the General Theory of Relativity, in which the behaviour of light is affected, as well as time and dimension, which is all very queasy indeed.

Nevertheless…

Einstein's theories have been verified by observation of objects in our solar system and beyond in the Universe. For example, in 1919, the General Theory of Relativity was empirically confirmed by measurements of the deflection of light from stars appearing close to the Sun during a total solar eclipse.

The principles of relativity seem very strange and hard to come to terms with in our everyday lives. We don't really have to, though, because at more normal speeds, such as those at which we are ever likely to travel, the effect is almost completely negligible. Time isn't going to slow down very much as we walk back from our lunch, for example, much as we might like it to. So we work with an approximation—a pretty good one—but still an approximation. We regard time as something we can trust, on the whole.

However, the implications of General Relativity are not so far away. The proper functioning of the satellite-based Global Positioning System (GPS), on which you probably rely from time to time, requires some corrections to be made to account for general relativity.

Meanwhile…

Modern science shows us the Universe is pretty

weird altogether. The quantum physicists tell us subatomic particles must, in effect, be able to communicate with each other instantaneously over immense distances, through a "non-local" phenomenon they call "entanglement." Hang on, though, doesn't that contravene what Einstein had to say about nothing being able to travel faster than the speed of light? Indeed it does. And so we have an issue reconciling these things. Have we sorted that out yet? It's not entirely clear. We still have to integrate fully these different interpretations. As statistician George Box said, "All models are wrong, but some are useful."

The Universe—Inside and outside

And what about the vastness of the Universe? It really is big, and it's old—around 13.798 billion years old apparently. Can we really make sense of that? And what about life on other planets? There seems now to be evidence on Mars of water existing billions of years ago, which could have supported microbial life.

The observable Universe is thought to be around 46.5 billion light years in radius. Now that's just the "observable" Universe—only the part we can see because the Universe is expanding quite rapidly and distant parts are receding from us faster than the speed of light, so we won't ever be able to see them. Because the Universe is expanding, astrophysicists can extrapolate back to its beginning in the now generally-accepted "Big Bang" theory. What was there before though, if anything? And what if there are other universes? There easily could be.

And why did any of it happen in the first place?

We tend to think the Big Bang theory means matter expanded out from the centre of the Universe. Actually, it doesn't mean that: It means that space itself expanded outward after the Big Bang. That's another lurch to the peculiar. So what did space expand into? It seems space itself has structure, which would correspond to a quantum theory of gravity. So it's that quantised structure that expanded after the Big Bang.

All very surprising and mysterious.

And yet…

We go about our lives on our little planet, conveniently thinking that our world is pretty much all there is for practical purposes. Of course, our energy comes from the star we call the Sun, and our seas are a bit affected by the moon, but other than that, we can ignore most of the rest of what's out there in space.

But doesn't it fill you with awe when you stop and think about the Universe? We are truly tiny—and the Earth is just a "pale blue dot," to quote Carl Sagan, and that's only when seen from as close a perspective as the edge of our Solar System.

The scale is staggering…

It has been estimated that there are more than 100 billion galaxies in the observable Universe. That sounds a huge number, but ponder this for a moment: That's the vastness on the outside. What about the vastness on the inside of us? Apparently there are 100 billion neurons in the human brain—a number comparable to the number of galaxies we can see in the Universe. And, of course, these neurons are interconnected by trillions of synapses. So, in some ways, we have as much complexity inside us as there is out there in the Universe.

There are 75–100 trillion cells and about $7x10^{27}$ atoms in the human body (based on a 70kg adult male) and about $3x10^{23}$ stars in the observable Universe. So there are around 20,000 times more atoms in our body than there are stars we can see in the Universe.

The thing is…

It's wise to have humility. We really don't understand that much, and we can't say how it all came to be. Perhaps we can't observe the system properly because we're part of it.

As Einstein said, "The scientist's religious feeling takes the form of a rapturous amazement at the harmony of natural law, which reveals an intelligence of such superiority that, compared with it, all the systematic thinking and acting of human beings is an utterly insignificant reflection."

A unifying theory?

Mystery is the doorway to understanding.

— From the *Tao Te Ching*, 1st Verse

If you're feeling a bit disorientated after a smattering of particle physics, the Universe, and Relativity, that was the idea, I'm afraid. I'm using my scientific training, a continuing interest in physics, and a gathering of a few facts to shake your certainties a little. I do apologise.

It helps foster change and growth when you loosen settled beliefs deliberately, just as bringing an attitude of wonder into everyday life is both healthy and helpful. Uncertainty reminds us that all is not always what it seems. Everything we know is at best an approximation—in fact, all we really experience is our own nervous system, not the world directly.

But I have another purpose…

We've touched on the two great theories of modern science: quantum physics and General Relativity, both of which have been robustly validated by scientific observation—and indeed, in the case of quantum physics particularly, are exploited in a wide range of everyday devices.

And yet…

Perhaps the biggest question in the field today is how to reconcile these two theories. All attempts to come up with a proven unifying theory have so far fallen short. There clearly is an integration of these principles because they simultaneously exist in the Universe. They must be unified in some way, perhaps in a field we can't experience and never will. Quantum physics and General Relativity may be special cases of a model we can't see because we're inside the system.

What perspectives are you missing in your situation because you're on the inside? As W. Edwards Deming said: "Help must come from outside because a system is not capable of understanding itself," or we could say more flippantly, "It's hard to read the label when you're inside the bottle," or "A fish doesn't know it's swimming in water." Such constraints afflict anyone operating on the inside of anything.

Learning and unlearning

Any time you feel absolutely certain of something, that's a sure sign that you have missed something.

— Richard Bandler

Even what we think we know for sure often turns out to be wrong. Either we didn't have the best information available and were wrong for that reason, or we did have the best information at the time, but it isn't the best information any more. So being ready and willing to unlearn is a good idea. Being open to doubt is healthy. Perhaps our assumptions are wrong or no longer valid.

Now…

Because our knowledge is held unconsciously, when we first question our thinking, it can feel very uncomfortable because we experience a deep-seated emotional reaction stemming from our ego. We may unreasonably resist the new information if we don't realise the emotional signals stem from the potential loss of something held to be true.

Open to possibility

It could be true: this new learning that we doubt, but are beginning to see evidence to support. Maybe it is right after all. So be open to possibility. You know how surprising some things turn out to be.

One of the lessons from the field of forecasting is that the future always turns out to be more surprising than anybody seriously predicted. Envisioned possible futures tend not to encompass what actually happens: They're not radical enough. The 2001 terrorist attacks on the United States in New York and Washington, DC, are examples of that. Nobody predicted such a world-changing event. They warned of the dangers of certain terrorist groups and individuals, but not such a cataclysm.

We can take another lesson from that… Because we like our comfort, we tend not to hear those voices that warn of problems coming. Always remember that the people who developed "conventional wisdom" were largely happy in their comfort zones, mostly avoiding responsibility. So they're more likely to be wrong than to be right. As Dagny Taggart famously says in Ayn Rand's *Atlas Shrugged*: "Place nothing—*nothing*—above the verdict of your own mind."

Knowing and knowing about

In order to learn to swim, you have to get in the water.

— Milton Erickson

Recognise the difference between knowing about something and knowing something.

For example, we can know about swimming in the sense of having some idea how people stay afloat and make forward progress in the water, but that's very different from successfully achieving the result ourselves. Knowing something inevitably requires the benefit of direct experience.

Humility in action

So…

As you go about your business, remember from time to time that what looks solid is mostly empty space, that everything you see is energy as well as matter, and that we are as complex on the inside as the Universe is on the outside. Remember that time, dimension, and speed are not quite the dependable quantities we imagine.

Test your knowledge.

Look out for two opposite dangers: overconfidence and playing small.

Act when it is time to act, in the knowledge that things are nothing like as certain as they might appear. Stay humble. As Mancur Olsen put it, the best we can hope for is a "fruitful fallacy," or as Peter Senge advises, "Approach an issue with humility."

The willingness to not know and to receive needed correction and overlooked information is a key hallmark of the true leader—almost a qualifying characteristic. Unfounded certainty is unconvincing for others and undermining for us.

You need your team to know you don't know and want their help. How else can they know they need to look out for missing information? They need to know that you will welcome them saying you might have overlooked something, made an error, or not noticed something important—or at least not round on them when they tell you.

That's the difference between the professional and the amateur: Professionals don't let issues land in their egos.

This principle is rather obvious skippering a yacht, for example. Get it wrong and you usually receive immediate and probably uncomfortable feedback from your environment. You need the crew to tell you things before you make a mistake, not after.

Otherwise you might hit the rocks.

In running an organisation, this principle is even more true, just a bit less obvious. It might be you that's out of step, not everyone else.

We know; we don't know.

That's life.

6

Strength and Courage

The commitment that makes the difference

Only one who has devoted himself to a cause with his whole strength and soul can be a true master. For this reason, mastery demands all of a person.

— Albert Einstein

Leadership takes commitment. In fact, change and progress require us to go beyond the point of no return. Otherwise, those around us will sense we are holding back and so will hold back too. That, after all, is what we would be manifesting: hesitation. So the world would hesitate. Those we seek to influence need to know we have let go of safety ourselves before they will join us.

I wonder if you recognise this experience: Have you acted beyond the possibility of reversing what you have done, like letting go of the side of the swimming pool to swim out of your depth? There is a kind of peace that comes from knowing you have acted fully and with intention. You've made your choice, and what's done is done. It's time to let go of the decision to act and cut all ties to it. The action can't be undone, and it only remains to see what transpires.

Of course, the outcome will be more useful if the choice of action was a wise one, but it doesn't matter how wise an action is if we don't take it. We won't lead or change anything unless we commit. The question might be: Does the desired outcome matter enough for us to put ourselves irrevocably into the fray?

Commitment is scary

If it matters, do it anyway. Overcome the resistance. If something seems frightening, that's all the more reason to do it. The fear is a signpost to the direction of your own growth.

Find a reason to propel yourself forward.

Here's one of mine...

Our youngest child has Autism, as I've mentioned already. He's doing pretty well, aged ten now, though there are plenty of challenges. Back in 2009 when we were looking for the most appropriate school for him, we visited the three special-needs schools in our area. One of them in particular provides for the most challenged children, some barely alive, in a sense. I find it heartbreaking to think about it even now, and I challenge anyone to visit such a place and not be profoundly affected, not to come away with a different sense of what really is a problem.

I remember one particular boy in a wheelchair. He would have been about five at the time, I think. His head was supported by part of his chair, and he couldn't speak. You might wonder, as I did, what's it like to be him?

I would express my experience a particular way now...

You meet soul to soul, because that's all there is. I remember this boy looking up at me, looking for love, I decided, because that's the only communication that makes any sense. At the time, I was working on my first book, which was well underway, but still I had this smack round the head: "David, if you can do something with your life, you bloody well should because not everyone has the same chance."

To be frank...

Thinking about people with immense challenges they didn't choose, I find it's easy to be angry at the state of the world and all its avoidable problems.

So any time I feel scared to follow through on something I've chosen to do, any time I hesitate, I think of my own family and also the boy in the wheelchair. Then my decision to act becomes easier. I do it for him because my life is easy and his is hard. I do what I do not out of anger, actually, but out of care for those who can't help themselves.

The courage to care

People don't care how much you know until they know how much you care.

— John Maxwell

Now we come to what I found frightening—terrifying, in fact: As I was working on *Relationship Mastery*, reflecting on my experiences and gathering together skills about relating to other people, it dawned on me that what rounded it all off was that deep human connection, which in fact is the most powerful force there is.

This is sometimes seen as an "undiscussable" or taboo subject, but that's all the more reason to discuss it…

The most powerful force available to us is love. Quite honestly, it's the only word strong enough for the power I'm talking about. Sometimes, I call it "care," but that's a ruse. "Care" is not really the right word. "Love" is the right word. Now, we need to watch what we mean here. Try Scott Peck's definition from *The Road Less Travelled*: "The will to extend one's self for the purpose of nurturing one's own or another's spiritual growth," or we could just say "growth." Do you notice that sounds quite like one of the definitions of leadership we opened with: "to contribute something to other people to help shape their future?"

Scott Peck goes on: "Since it requires the extension of ourselves, love is always either work or courage. If an act is not one of work or courage, then it is not an act of love. There are no exceptions."

So…

I put a chapter on Love into my first book. It's a short chapter, because I didn't think I knew very much about the subject, but I did know it was crucial and I couldn't leave it out. That would have been a disservice to my readers. While it was a short chapter, it was still quite long enough to be terrifying to write.

That's the most frightening thing I've ever done in my working life: put a chapter on love in my book. I'm an engineer in the West of Scotland, for goodness sake. What was I thinking of? (If the meaning of that geographical reference isn't clear to you, let's just say West of Scotland men are not usually known for their feminine side.)

But here's what made my mind up…

I said to myself, suppose it was my last chance to say what I had to say. Remember Tolstoy's Ivan Ilyitch: Don't die with your music still in you.

Funnily enough…

The chapter on love is often the one readers look at first. Not so long ago, for example, I met with a director of a civil engineering business. I left him with a copy of the book, as is the way. He wrote to me later: "I haven't started reading your book yet, but have flicked through it and enjoyed some of the quotes. Have to say these are very well chosen and very applicable. I especially enjoyed the one under the love chapter!"

What's the quote?

You'll recognise this immediately…

I may be able to speak the languages of men and even of angels, but if I have no love,
my speech is no more than a noisy gong or a clanging bell.

— 1 Corinthians 13

The passage from *St Paul's Letter to the Corinthians* that contains these lines is often read at marriage ceremonies, as if it mostly applies to romantic love. In my view, that's not what St Paul was writing about. He was addressing a much more general theme: the central importance of love in all human interaction and the resulting emptiness if it's lacking.

Through noticing people being drawn to that which I found most frightening to do, I've learned that it's when you're acting at the edge of certainty that people are most ready to follow and when you are, therefore, truly leading. It's only when you're at least a little scared, that you're really a leader—no use being in your comfort zone then. As Steven Pressfield writes, "The more important a call or action is to our soul's evolution, the more resistance we will feel towards pursuing it" because of the perceived threat to the ego.

So…

In completing my book *Relationship Mastery*, I realised St Paul's sentiment is all you really need to remember, even in the results-orientated business world with which we are so familiar. That's what my red box of books was telling me back then.

How many noisy gongs and clanging bells are in your life? Which ones are you ringing yourself?

Now, obviously…

When things are difficult in organisations, of course we need to be resolute, reduce numbers, and make other difficult decisions, but it'll be easier in the long run if we come from a place of caring.

Now you might be thinking…

If I do this love thing, won't that make me a doormat? Someone asked just that question of Marianne Williamson, one of the authorities in this area, during a talk she gave in Manchester a few years ago. She was moving among the audience, taking questions with a roving microphone at the time. "No!" she said emphatically, "A doormat is what you are now." She continued, "There's something about people who really live this that says don't mess with me." Marianne can handle herself, and you wouldn't mess with her.

I was convinced.

I hope you are too.

Fear and love

We're so afraid, many of us, to talk about the subject of "love," and yet it's absolutely key to understanding leadership, as well as change. In some contexts, we avoid talking about it at all. The irony of that is it's the very power we need to understand and harness if we are to move forward. So by dismissing the subject, we may be neglecting the only perspective that can resolve our situation. We have a serious cultural problem here if we can't discuss what we need to discuss.

It's tempting to ease our embarrassment by thinking of "care" and "compassion" instead, but neither of these words quite covers the whole sentiment. These words allude more to sympathy for someone in difficulty, which is an aspect certainly, but we also need the part of the meaning that refers to gain—the positive nurturing of an individual (or oneself) to be all that he or she can be.

For many years, I accepted the idea that we have only two fundamental emotions: fear and love. Every other emotion boils down to one of these two. The art then is to find ways of responding to a situation from a place of love rather than a place of fear. We may not always find it easy to have the presence of mind to do that in the moment, but still, that's what will help us.

More recently, thanks principally to Marianne Williamson, I have understood this in a more powerful way. It's not, in fact, that there are two fundamental emotions—fear and love. There is only one fundamental emotion: love. Fear is simply an absence of love. So fear is emptiness—the dark—whereas love is energy—the light—just as dark is the absence of light, not really its opposite at all. Similarly, the opposite of love isn't hate; it's indifference—emptiness.

So here's the bizarre thing...

The inescapable logic is, in fearing to talk about love—and don't we run from that subject, especially in organisations?—we're afraid of talking about the antidote to fear. That's our ego at work.

And so we are stuck. Our culture (and our ego) keeps us stuck in fear. In fact, some of our institutions, including some of our religious ones, are set up to sustain exactly that. But I really don't believe that's what the Universe—or anybody's God, including yours or mine—intends. It just doesn't stack up psychologically. Why would our Spirit want us to be shut down in fear? It doesn't make any sense. If we were meant to live in fear, then God or the Universe would have to be intent on resisting evolution. That's not how it looks to me.

Instead...

As Erich Fromm said, “Love is the only sane and satisfactory answer to the problem of human existence” and the ultimate answer, therefore, to every question. The only issue is in what specific way.

Indeed, as Steven Pressfield writes: “The ego doesn’t want us to evolve. The ego runs the show right now. It likes things just the way they are,” whereas for the Self, “The supreme emotion is love. Union and mutual assistance are the imperatives of life. We are all in this together.” He goes on: “Our job, as souls on this mortal journey, is to shift the seat of our identity from the lower realm to the upper, from the ego to the Self.”

At a much more prosaic level, Deming believed, “Wherever there is fear, there will be wrong figures” because people will always manipulate the reported numbers if they are sufficiently scared. Bear that in mind if you want to see what’s really going on in a challenging situation.

I recall someone senior in an engineering business revealing to me that he thought they had a problem with stress in their organisation. A few moments later, I mentioned something about caring for employees. He shot back: “Oh. We wouldn’t want them to think that we cared.” (He wasn’t joking.) Well, there’s an explanation for the stress right there.

The stages of life

Carl Jung talked about stages of development in

life. Wayne Dyer articulates a version of this that is particularly clear. There are four stages: The first is called "athlete," and lasts up until perhaps age 20. In this stage, we're concerned with our appearance. Next is "warrior," which is all about what we can get and winning. Then we have "statesperson," where we think more about what we can give and how we can serve others. In the fourth stage, we may recognise ourselves as spiritual beings having a human experience rather than human beings having a spiritual experience. The key point for us here is that an orientation of what you can give and how you can serve is a state reached beyond an orientation of what you can get. That is to say, acting as a "statesperson" involves a greater degree of maturity.

That doesn't necessarily mean we must aim for that statesperson state at all times. More likely, we need a balance between the warrior (the egoist) and the statesperson (the altruist) in our lives. Too much warrior, and we disconnect ourselves from other people and preclude the opportunities that come from collaboration as well as from contributing to the community on which we ultimately depend. Too much statesperson, and we risk being exploited by the unscrupulous, and our ventures may become slack and inefficient.

Two questions (at least) arise: How much are you a warrior and how much a statesperson? What's the balance in your life?

And what do you want your team to be? Some organisations see fit to push their people into warrior mode all the time, competing with each other—akin to gladiators, when you think about it. The trouble with that is they can't be expected to place their own needs second to the greater good. That'll have consequences when the organisation has to change and adapt because its people won't take risks.

Be careful about the signals you're sending about whether you want your people to act as warriors or statespeople. And of course, the most important signal is your own example.

The place of ultimate safety

Abraham Maslow, in his Hierarchy of Needs, identified the need for physical and psychological safety as one of the most fundamental needs of human beings, second only to food, shelter, and so on. In other words, like animals in general, we are a fearful species. It keeps us alive. However, it's also limiting.

Whenever you're faced with a situation with people that isn't as you would like it to be, ask yourself where the fear exists and what its nature is. Who is afraid and what are they afraid of? What are you afraid of? What can you do about it? Bearing in mind that the universal antidote to fear is love, how does that translate into the practical reality of the situation?

Bill Clinton, former President of the United States, said of Nelson Mandela and his willingness to forgive his captors from the apartheid regime in South Africa: "Mandela understood that unless he forgave completely, he would never truly be free." If he remained a victim, he would not succeed in freeing his country. Acting from fear, he could not be free. In fact, his love for his fellow man overcame his fear and fuelled his capacity for forgiveness.

Leadership comes not from fear, but from love, which gives us courage, all the safety we need, and ultimately all the safety that is any use—the only thing that matters in the end. To echo Einstein, true mastery, including leadership mastery, requires all of your being, including your love. Then others will follow.

The moment one definitely commits oneself, then providence moves too.

— W. H. Murray

Leading with courage

In organisations, having strength and courage means taking unequivocal action. Often, what happens instead is hesitancy and wariness. Some caution before commitment is appropriate, but there comes a time when we must move forward and abandon the security of our starting point. Otherwise, we will never truly set off and, through our weakness, we will inhibit the contribution of those we lead.

Blind commitment isn't the answer. What we need instead is "an eye for the main chance," coupled with the nerve to proceed at the necessary pace when circumstances are right. As W. H. Murray, inspired by Goethe, wrote, "Boldness has genius, power, and magic in it."

Leaders care; leaders commit.

7

Learning and Growth

Adapting organisations

The problem with most organisations is that they are governed by mediocre ideas.

— Bill O'Brien, CEO, Hanover Insurance (retired)

We don't need to think about leadership and change for very long before we realise both are inextricably tied up with learning—our own and that of our associates and our organisations. By organisations, we can mean all of businesses, public institutions, schools, families, countries even, and more, up to and including the world. In all of these, collective learning and change and growth takes place—or not, as the case may be. One of the most important roles of a leader is to stimulate an organisation to learn and change with the times.

The living organisation

Organisations are not, of course, separate, living beings, and yet it's often convenient to look at them as if they are, as Arie de Gues sets out in *The Living Company*. This is especially true for organisations changing and evolving or in circumstances where they need to be.

We can look at many situations from the perspective of learning: What does the organisation need to learn in order to deliver the project, implement the service, or whatever? That's not usually how we look at it, though, and so a different viewpoint is often illuminating. More often, we talk as if people—and the organisation—can remain unchanged and still complete the piece of work they are about to undertake. In most cases, that's simply not true. Indeed as a friend involved in participatory leadership and community engagement work, Tim Merry, put it neatly, "When we're doing something new, the only way we can tell how well we're doing is by how much we're growing."

Organisational learning doesn't happen of its own accord. It's not really the natural order of things. We might think it would be, but it isn't. Just as individual people tend to learn most in their younger years as a feature of human nature, so too organisations tend to adapt more slowly as they age. Active steps are needed to overcome this inertia.

This also matters from a personal perspective…

If you're in step with an organisation that isn't really learning, it means you're being left behind by your industry, because we live in a fast-changing world.

Human beings have clearly evolved over the millennia. From one lifetime to the next, gradual change kept pace with changing circumstances, or adequately so anyway. That's how it used to be. Any individual perhaps didn't need to evolve in her own lifetime—mature, yes, but not evolve.

Nowadays, it's different: Life expectancies are longer and at the same time, the world is changing much faster. Five thousand years ago, in contrast, we know that our ancestors lived in much the same way for generation after generation, for hundreds of years. It's not like that now. We need to evolve in our lifetimes if we're going to keep pace. And so do our organisations.

A model of organisational learning

Peter Senge sets out a very useful framework for understanding organisational learning in his highly regarded book *The Fifth Discipline*. This is a very important piece of the jigsaw that we really can't do without.

To get an organisation to learn, we need five things in place…

Shared vision

The organisation needs to know its goals, where it is aiming to get to, clearly—sufficiently clearly so that if it arrives there, it is capable of knowing that it has. That is the test of a sufficiently clear vision. Flippantly: Would you recognise it if it showed up?

The shared vision needs to be one that everybody supports, or at least most do. Something handed down from on high is no use. Also, neither "make such and such a return on capital" nor "increase sales by x%" is a vision. These are objectives. As management writer Peter Drucker said, "Making a profit is to organisations as breathing is to people. You need to do it to stay alive, but if you think that's all there is to life, you might have missed something."

In fact, creating a vision that all involved completely agree with isn't realistic and would probably be counter-productive. We can more accurately say the vital ingredient is the sharing (and respecting) of the vision by all concerned. In other words, the key enabling step is making time for everyone to talk about their aspirations and how they dovetail together in the context of the organisation and the vision they hold for it—what the common ground seeks to achieve.

As Mary Parker-Follett said back in the 1930s: "Collective clarity of purpose is the invisible leader." Get the shared vision right, and people will lead themselves.

Mental models

For organisations to learn and operate beyond "better-than-mediocre ideas," they need agreed and understood ways of talking about what they do. Peter Drucker said the question that most needs to be asked, and yet is least asked, is: "What is the theory of our business?"—meaning what are the models through which we understand and develop how our organisation works? As he put it, "A good theory of the thing is usually pretty important."

However, we tend to hold our models unconsciously, especially the more important and significant parts, because they're part of our unconscious competences. That means that we are liable to assume, without thinking, that we are operating from the same model as someone else when that may not be the case at all.

Moreover…

If our models are challenged by someone who sees things a different way, we may well feel deeply threatened because we have so much invested in our worldview. We may also have limited conscious awareness of the specific cause of the unease—rather, just a vague sense of threat putting us on the defensive. We see this in many, if not all, professions where new ideas are often met with a great deal of resistance by vested interest groups because to accept them would upset the established precedence. As a consequence, management teams and leaders may be very unwilling to examine their own assumptions or even acknowledge such assumptions exist.

All professions rest on a model of how things work: engineering, medicine, law, and accountancy, for instance. All these models have a very great deal invested in them so when contradictions arise within or between them, it can be quite unsettling.

In contrast, wise leaders and enlightened professionals are prepared to "suspend" their assumptions for examination—to make them visible. They accept they may not know or may not be right.

Team dialogue

We need effective and honest communication and a process of learning together—good relationships, in other words. Teams learn best as a unit. We can send all the members of a team on a training course, one after the other, and the team as a whole and the organisation still won't learn anything. The process of sharing experience is vital to collective growth.

For adaptation and change, we need rather more supportive interaction and rather less adversarial discussion. In many circumstances, learning requires a generative type of conversation in which meaning builds on meaning, in the manner of David Bohm's principles of dialogue. On the other hand, when it comes time for action, a bit of hierarchy is useful and more of a "skilful discussion" is appropriate, which means a conversation about a specific aim with tangible outcomes, keeping the principles of dialogue in mind.

Personal mastery

Personal mastery requires us to see clearly and to "own" in what happens around us, the component that we created, and not blame other people or other things when our actions don't work out—to take responsibility, in other words. Without that, we block the feedback from our environment that we need to receive in order to learn. As Joshua Cooper Ramo says in his book *The Age of the Unthinkable*, "If we are not seeing things properly, we have no hope of any sort of breakthrough." Unless we deal in reality, there is no chance of progress.

One of the most important things a leader can do is create the circumstances where people take responsibility and see things as they really are. The best, or even the only, way is by our own example in accepting when we've made a mistake. That's not always our first response, of course. (As long as it's our second, though, we'll get away with our weakness.)

Systems thinking

The fifth enabler of organisational learning is systems thinking, meaning the ability to discern cause and effect even if separated in both time and space. The consequences of a decision and action taken now and in a particular place may not appear until sometime later—perhaps years later—and in some other location, perhaps very distant. We must appreciate the dynamic and interdependent nature of things in order to be successful cultivators of organisational learning and change.

For example…

A familiar scenario is when an organisation introduces a new product or service. Some issues arise that need to be resolved, and of course, that requires resources. The normal response within the organisation is to take people off other upstream product and service development work, transferring them to fix the issues affecting the new product. It's likely that, fairly quickly, the difficulties will be resolved. The problem, of course, is that the upstream projects suffer as a consequence of the resources shift. Those future projects, when eventually introduced, will have even more problems, requiring even more significant emergency resources.

An organisation can easily end up in a vicious cycle in which it descends into a chaos of "fire fighting" that's very difficult for orderly management and leadership to overcome. Those who shout loudest tend to hold sway.

Often too, the problem is compounded by praise heaped on the fire-fighting heroes who successfully rescue the situation, thus of course highlighting what the truly valued behaviour is, thereby reinforcing the pattern.

To break the cycle…

The systemically thinking leader needs to have the presence of mind to protect future projects and bring independent assistance in to resolve the current problems or in some other way decouple the two loops—one loop being the "symptomatic solution" (the transfer of resources to solve short-term problems) and the other the "fundamental solution" (the application of adequate resources to upstream product development).

This pattern of two interacting loops, illustrated below, appears in many contexts. As an archetypal pattern, it's called "shifting the burden" because the action of applying the symptomatic solution usually makes the fundamental problem worse. This scenario is endemic in organisations and society at large. Once you start looking, you see the pattern everywhere.

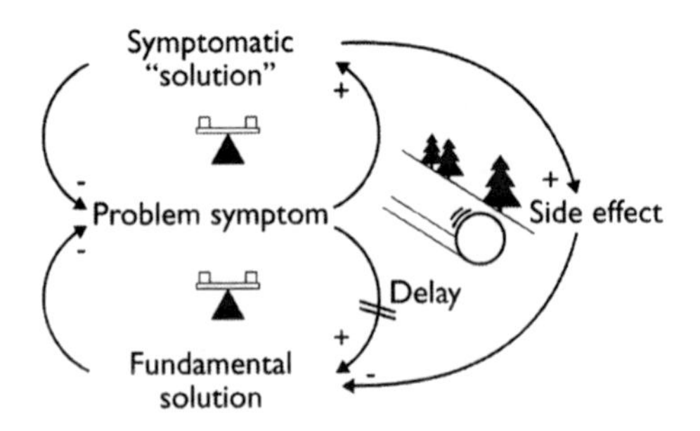

The see-saw symbols indicate loops that will reach equilibrium through negative feedback. The rolling snowball indicates a loop with positive reinforcement, which, left to its own devices, will increase without limit.

Another archetypal pattern is "limits to growth," shown below, in which growing actions of one kind or another produce growth in a condition such as the performance of a business. As the condition changes, however, consequences of that change create effects slowing down or even reversing the change. These limiting effects are caused by constraints.

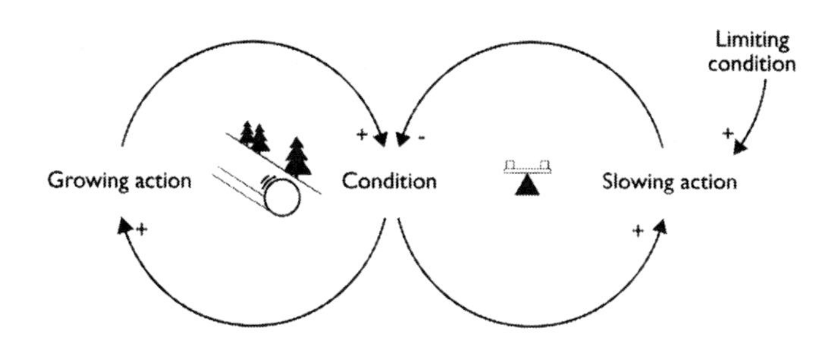

Unfortunately, we often seek to improve matters by driving the growing actions harder—making more sales calls or demanding more work from the team, for example—when the more mindful response would be to reflect on the limiting factors and do something about them. In a growing business, that might entail developing new participative leadership styles to spread the management burden beyond the core group, for instance. Recognising and addressing this particular pattern of behaviour represents an opportunity for many developing organisations.

"Shifting the burden" and "limits to growth" are just two examples of systemic structure. There are many more.

In general...

To change and learn successfully, an organisation needs to be mindful of these systemic effects. Otherwise, it risks doing exactly the wrong thing by merely responding to events as they arise.

Organisational learning on a larger scale

To summarise, for our organisation to learn, we need five things in place:

- Shared vision
- Mental models
- Team dialogue
- Personal mastery
- Systems thinking

If any one of these is missing, the learning and adapting process is disabled. So, for example, if there's a great deal of blame going on in our organisation, we can be pretty sure it isn't learning anything.

Peter Senge would also say, "Don't wait for the

CEOs." In other words, "pick yourself," to use Seth Godin's phrase, if you want something different to happen.

Now…

This perspective of organisational learning is usually applied to, literally, organisations, but it also applies to enterprises, meaning organisations working together. If the enterprise is going to learn, we need the same five disciplines. And if we have too many "games" being played between the organisations—too much adversarial behaviour going on, too much debate and not enough dialogue—the enterprise won't learn. So our business might win the game—we might succeed in optimising our part of the system—but the enterprise as a whole might go out of business. In a sense, that's what happened to the banks in the "credit crunch" of 2008 or to the record industry when online distribution of music became the norm.

On a larger scale, thinking of countries as organisations of a kind, we can see that the business of modern politics tends to make a mockery of the personal mastery element, in particular, and so countries learn only at a rather slow pace. That's a drawback of the Western approach to democracy: Finding differences, as required by the practice of professional politics, interferes with the ability of the nation as an entity to learn. Internationally, we can see why the notion of countries and how they typically interact may preclude the world from learning to solve its global problems. All five of the prerequisites for collective learning are shaky at best.

Organisational learning in practice

Having found this whole area of organisational learning extremely useful, I followed my principle of going to the source and so attended Peter Senge's programme on leadership a couple of years ago. I recount this because the experience itself conveys some important points about leadership…

First of all…

Peter has been running his leadership and systems thinking programme for more than 25 years, which is an impressive statistic that conveys something of its significance. (It seems all the well-known thought leaders have been doing what they do for a long time. That's worth bearing in mind when initial progress on a change effort seems slow.)

I asked what was important in the development of organisational learning as a topic and for the success of his book *The Fifth Discipline*. Peter said—significantly, I felt—"It's all about community." In other words, building a face-to-face community and peer-to-peer networks around an idea or a philosophy is what makes the difference. It also implies that relationships are important.

So…

Now we know how to get organisations to learn and to change and to grow.

Not quite…

We are likely to encounter obstacles, and they could be big ones.

Resistance to learning and "skilled incompetence"

In individuals, insanity is rare; but in groups, parties, nations, and epochs, it is the rule.

— Friedrich Nietzsche

Read the literature on organisational learning, and you'll find compelling descriptions of how fear or embarrassment impedes learning by individuals and teams. By constantly turning the focus away from our own behaviour to that of others, we bring learning to a grinding halt, to paraphrase Chris Argyris, the key authority in this area, whose Harvard Business Review paper *Teaching Smart People How To Learn* is a classic. When something doesn't turn out as expected, it's a very human reaction to seek to cover up the failing—to step past it somehow—and then cover up that we've done that. Finally, we make rules that we don't talk about these things. We make the subject "undiscussable," to use the term Chris Argyris coined.

The truth is, though…

If we can't talk about something, we can be sure we need to.

Repeat the covering up a few times, and we soon enter the territory of what some call "skilled incompetence"—artful ways of consistently protecting ourselves from threat at the expense of disconnecting ourselves from feedback. In short, our egos make us resistant and get in the way of our learning. We engage in defensive reasoning. Actually, we tend to overdo the fear and the embarrassment beyond the likely consequences.

I remember having this attitude to training courses—a reticence about being taught something I didn't know. It was a completely stupid reaction, of course, because nobody else was expecting me to know. After all, if I already had the knowledge, what was the point of taking the course? I'm over all that now, I'm glad to say, but it's a manifestation of the same pride (ego) that stops organisations from learning in everyday work, all over the world.

The typical organisation expresses "espoused theories" about how things are done. An observer may often see that the actual "theories in use" are quite different. Dee Hock speaks of "the chasm between how institutions profess to function and how they actually do." The theories in use and the values that underpin them are held unconsciously, of course. That's why we can be so unaware of saying one thing and doing another. Until the organisation faces up to its actual theories in use and becomes conscious of them, little will change.

If you have a sense that your organisation is talking about one thing while reality is doing something else, you can be sure you've got skilled incompetence going on, and if you're actively stopping your people talking about an awkward subject, you're definitely heading for a fall.

Now, ironically and challengingly for me...

The relationship skills question I made my focus for a while, and to which I will set out an answer in the next chapter, is one of the great undiscussable subjects. It's not polite to suggest we might have something to learn in arguably the most important skill area of our lives. I suspect part of the problem is that in showing people how they can be skilful in interpersonal relationships, we take away their last, best excuse: They can no longer blame other people. The familiar lament, "If it weren't for the people, it would be easy," no longer applies, or at least not in the same way.

But here's the thing...

If you talk to people about leadership, there comes a moment when you can gather them round and say, "Can I let you into a secret about leadership... You have to relate to people."

American journalist, Herbert Agar, accurately described resistance to learning. He said: "The truth which makes people free is for the most part the truth which they prefer not to hear." (Actually, he said "men," but I've made the sentiment gender-neutral.) Freedom is frightening and embarrassing: Oh my God... We might have to step up.

The thing is...

The world doesn't know what it needs, and it doesn't

know what it doesn't know. That's why change requires skill in marketing and spreading ideas.

What have you found when you turn up with answers that you know can really help people? What's been the response when you've tried that? Some version of indifference is the usual reaction, typically directed at the individual. "Who the hell are you?" might be an appropriate summary. And it hurts, especially if we let it land in our ego. (Of course, when we're challenged in this way, our leadership is truly tested—when we need to know our inner purpose, to have our own map.)

But if we realise it's all actually about the egos, theirs and ours, then the reaction makes sense, and we can begin to see how to deal with it.

Noticing ego

Do you have an ego?

Well, of course you do, but it's ironic that your ego itself causes a twinge of discomfort when that question is asked. We all have an ego, though. If we didn't, we'd have great difficulty functioning. We wouldn't have proper awareness of ourselves as a separate individual. It's an unconscious thing mostly—part of the animal brain we talked about earlier. The problem comes when we're unaware of the effect of ego. As Carl Jung said, "The unconscious... is dangerous only when our conscious attitude to it becomes hopelessly false."

Here's a little example...

One day, I decided to go for a swim at the local swimming pool. I checked the timetable on the leisure centre website for the times when the pool was available for the general public, or I thought I did anyway. When I arrived at the pool, the lady behind the reception desk said very politely: "I'm sorry, but the pool closes at six o'clock every Monday."

She must have made a mistake, I thought… "Are you sure? The website says it's open."

She confirmed the pool was definitely closed.

I was all for blaming something, so I said… "I think the website must be wrong." I felt my body (my unconscious) reacting to the dissonance between what the receptionist said and what I believed to be true. (The effect of ego is almost a physical thing—the beginnings of the freeze, fight, or flight response.)

The receptionist astutely said she didn't know anything about the website, avoiding meeting me on that field. I managed to recognise reality, but not responsibility, and left. On this occasion, I had the presence of mind—just—to realise my unconscious might be wrong and to suppress the rising reaction in me. I managed to avoid getting into a ridiculous argument about whether the pool was open or not. Of course, I had simply made a mistake. The website was perfectly correct. It said the pool closed at six o'clock.

This is a trivial example, but the pattern is typical. Such are the consequences of ego. This is a problem we all face—our ego blocks feedback or information from which we need to learn.

And thus, in his considered view,
what did not suit—could not be true.
— Christian Morgenstern

It's all about the egos

When it comes to learning and change, what you really need to remember is: It's all about the egos.

Well-known authorities on organisational learning advocate various clever intellectual and conversational techniques to overcome the problem of defensive reasoning. If we handle meetings in a certain way, use certain processes, and say the right things at the right times, we'll neutralise the fear and embarrassment and lead our teams into honestly appraising their experience. The key part of that is to express our assumptions and invite scrutiny of them.

It's all rather complicated to work at this cerebral level, though. Fortunately there's an easier way, if we have the courage to take it…

The secret of promoting learning in organisations is to manage the egos and become truly mindful of our own. We must learn to notice when our ego is affecting our response, when we have an urge to blame someone or something else for what's just happened when we know inside that it's really our own doing.

The question is how to deal with the egos—our own

and others'. Well, it turns out there's a straightforward answer—something that's even more powerful than the effect of ego. Rather than trying to tackle the issue cerebrally, as is usually attempted, the way forward is to bring our humanity to bear.

Human connection is the answer to the conundrum of the learning organisation—the need to nullify defensive reasoning and skilled incompetence. Trying to handle anti-learning in organisations intellectually is very difficult. It's much easier and more reliable to use deep human connection. Therein lies a vital role of the leader: to overcome ego with humanity.

Warrior or statesperson?

When it comes to promoting learning and change in organisations, the statesperson will have more success than the warrior, to use Carl Jung's frame of reference, because the Self is at work rather than the ego.

If you're a warrior out for what you can get at the expense of the greater good, or if a significant number of people in your organisation are, then ego effects are going to predominate and you'll end up with an organisation which doesn't adapt very well to changing circumstances. Unbridled competition will take you down this path, for sure.

Someone with a statesperson mentality, on the other hand, is likely to use their attitude of service to promote the interconnections within an organisation on which innovation and adaptation depend. They will be more effective collaborators.

So…

Just as for the individual for whom the passage of life and the progression from warrior to statesperson involves coming to terms with the ego, the same holds true in organisations. Successful learning, change, and growth require that ego be understood, respected, and pacified.

Learning and change is (almost) all about the egos.

8

Interpersonal Success

Relating to people

Only in relationship with other people can we be fulfilled and enabled to grow.

— Martin Buber

Any act of leadership and any effort to stimulate change and evolution—outside of ourselves, that is—whether on a small or large scale, can only happen through connection with other people. Our ability to build effective relationships quickly, easily, and reliably, and to maintain them through time, is an essential skill for that and many other reasons. We may also need to foster effective relationships amongst team members and other people in general.

A community or organisation is a system we might hope to influence, and the interconnections within that system consist of human relationships. Those are the linkages that bind the system together and give it resilience, or cause it to fail when they weaken or break. So if we work on the relationships, including our own, we strengthen the system, make it more adaptable, and increase our ability to influence it.

We learn the necessary relationship skills primarily by trial and error, of course, and this method is not without its drawbacks. Progress is slow, for a start, and mistakes are expensive and their consequences sometimes difficult to rectify. The truth is, we can radically improve matters if we make use of appropriate insights and adopt a structured approach.

Sadly…

There is a gulf between what happens in this area and what could happen. Collectively, we're just not that skilful at dealing with people—at least not compared with how effective we could be. The difference is like turning the lights on in a darkened room. Suddenly, we see clearly what's going on, and the great potential for different outcomes everywhere becomes apparent.

So a methodical approach to relationship skills just makes everything else easier. Most of what we do involves dealing with people, whether at home, at work, or anywhere else. However, we grow up thinking that there's really no way to approach such an important skill area systematically. In fact, with the right insights, we can deal tangibly with what seems like an intangible area. The key is being prepared to dip into the psychological tools and timeless wisdom that make the difference, as well as being ready to learn and grow in ourselves as we do so—in other words, being amenable to change.

Relationship mastery

Of course, we are always evolving and using our experiences, almost moment to moment, to learn and grow. However, insights that illuminate the feedback cycle can accelerate the process and save us from painful mistakes.

We can choose to expect change in our approach to other people and, in fact, to welcome it. We might call this a philosophy of "relationship mastery." We benefit from applying an attitude of mastery and learning to our dealings with people in our professional and personal relationships. Method helps. My particular prescription is in my earlier book *Relationship Mastery: A Business Professional's Guide*, which sets out an in-depth, systematic approach—a formula if you like—to develop our ability to relate to other people. There are twelve elements in the system, each of which is a study in itself.

Relationship mastery is both a component of leadership and an area crying out for change. To succeed in sharing knowledge and learning, we need to be effective in relationships. In fact, the ability to connect with people and convey the right insight at the right moment is in many ways what makes the difference between having knowledge and imparting wisdom—wisdom being in a sense the currency of leadership.

However, relationship mastery does not mean being on wonderful terms with everybody. It might, in fact, at times involve being mindful of who we may upset on our chosen path and making a conscious choice to accept that cost.

That said…

In outline, the twelve elements are as follows…

Attention to others

For many of us, the first step in improving our results is paying rather less attention to what's going on for us and rather more to what's going on for other people. Keep what we want in mind, yes, but follow with that rather than lead with it. This principle of "attention to others" sums up the whole of Dale Carnegie's classic *How to Win Friends and Influence People*.

Attending to others sounds simple, but it takes discipline, practice, and presence of mind to achieve consistently. It begins with diligent listening—deep listening even—to hear, see, or feel what's really going on for someone, which our senses may reveal is quite different from what their words are saying.

But it goes beyond that…

Attention to others means focusing on what the other person needs next, what matters to them, and what we can do to assist. Actually succeeding in helping them may not be essential. Making their needs and wants central to our concerns may be enough. As Seth Godin says, "People want to be sure you heard what they said—they're less focused on whether you *do* what they said."

Asking great questions—generally open ones (starting with "what," "where," "when," "how," "who," and "which")—and keeping our ideas and opinions out of the conversation form the basis of this approach.

Despite what we may have been told at a younger

age, it's best to avoid "why" questions because they can sound judgmental and anyway tend to be vague or weak. We can always ask a more directed question like: "What was your reason for…?" or "What was your intention in…?" or "What was important to you about…?" instead of "why?" We will get a more useful, more measured, wiser answer if we do.

Attitude

We need to bring to our relationships an appropriate attitude, which is in turn determined by what we choose to believe. Some choices are more conducive to effective relationships and successful leadership than others. Of course, it's not just a matter of choosing these beliefs in our thinking: We need to live them as well—not just when it's easy, but when it's hard.

Our beliefs need not be universal truths. Well, they might be, but that's not the point. Rather, choose them with faith that the choice will lead to better results. Here is a set of beliefs that work well: We have seen some of them already…

Everyone is entitled to his worldview

We each see the world differently, based on our experiences to date, as well as our upbringing and culture. Depending on how much we have in common, our worldviews or "maps" of the world will be different to a greater or lesser degree. As Alfred Korzybski famously put it back in the 1930s, "The map is not the territory," meaning our worldview is only our approximation of the world itself.

So…

Others have a right to see the world the way they see it. That doesn't mean we have to agree with them—not at all. It does mean we must accept that they have a right to their map. If we respect that, we will get better results, even in a leadership role. Acknowledging the right of team members to see things the way they see them, even if we make clear our view is different, will still derive a benefit.

The effect of our communication is our responsibility

When we accept responsibility for the effect of our communication (or lack of communication) and do something about it when the outcome isn't what we wanted or expected, we will gain over time. The opposite is blaming the listener for the weakness in what we said with: "You've missed the point," "They don't get it," or "You've got the wrong end of the stick." Instead, say something like: "I'm sorry. I can't have been clear. Let me try that again."

Mind and body are interconnected

In the Western world, we tend to act as if our brain and our head determine everything. That really isn't the case. There's a strong connection between what happens with our bodies and what happens in our heads. Changing ourselves physically in some way—

just by moving, for example—will change our thoughts. For instance, if we stand upright with our held tilted up towards the ceiling and force a smile onto our face, it's hard to hold a state of depression.

Flexible people have more influence

Flexible people get better results, on average, most of the time. The more "cards we have to play," the more likely it is we will have the right one for a particular scenario. So, the art is to work on our flexibility, all the time—and that could be in our thinking, our being, or our behaviour. The flexibility to change our physical posture or cause other people to change theirs can be enough to unlock an impasse.

People's intentions are positive for them, and for us too, if we choose to see it

People have a reason for doing what they do or being how they are. The consequences may be inconvenient for us or worse, but they have a positive intention. Figure that out, and we are halfway to devising a plan to meet their needs in a different way—one that is more amenable to us.

What would need to be true for them to behave the way they are behaving?

Taking this further, we can choose to believe people we find difficult have shown up in our lives to teach us something, even though they don't know it. What lesson of life are we being offered as we ponder how to deal with them successfully?

We have everything we need

We can make whatever choices we like. We don't actually need anything from anyone else to do so. As Milton Erickson believed, we already have within us everything we need. We are already enough.

Results are feedback, whatever they are

When we take action, we may achieve the outcome we hope for; then again, we may not. If we don't, the results we get are just feedback that we haven't yet found the right approach. They're not failures as such. Failure only happens if we give up. Treat any outcome as feedback from which to learn and adjust.

There's always a way to proceed

There is a solution to every problem; it's just a question of finding it. Have faith. This belief comes from Virginia Satir, who did groundbreaking work with families. If there was a problem with a family member, she believed that meant there was a problem with the whole family. Organisations are more than a little similar. If there is a "problem" person, sure, we need to act, but at another level, that person may be our teacher, in the sense that they are reflecting something about the company. As we learn to deal with them, we grow and evolve as a leader.

We can learn from other people

If others can do a particular thing or be a particular way, chances are we can too if we study in detail what they are doing and emulate their actions. To be successful, we will probably need to include the non-verbal side of what they do as well as what they say: their posture, movement, tone of voice, how they control their environment, and so on.

Who we are is more significant than what we do

The most significant aspect of our being is really who we are, or perhaps what we are. In achieving influence, that's much more significant than what we do. Our sense of identity has the biggest effect.

Energy follows attention

What we focus on grows because our energy flows into it. For that reason, it's wise to express our desires in terms of what we want rather than an absence of what we don't want—saying it the way we want it and being careful what we wish for.

The unconscious mind always takes the best choice available

Our unconscious mind can be relied upon to select the best option amongst those available, according to the criteria it applies. We never deliberately select an inferior choice. It might seem like that to others looking on, but that just means they aren't seeing all the criteria.

So…

If we find ways of increasing the number of choices available, we can essentially leave it to a person to select the best one. We can let go of the issue without dragging a decision out of them, once we have opened their eyes to other possibilities. If that means we have to forego the satisfaction of seeing the outcome, so be it.

Self-control

To relate effectively to other people, we need to be calm—ideally the calmest person in the room or in the situation. Then we will have the most influence. In "Purpose and Resilience," we covered a simple meditative procedure to strengthen our calmness.

Several people I know, whom I would regard as having great presence, meditate on a daily basis. Some are very successful indeed in business, others in mediating conflict. They say they couldn't do the work they do if they didn't meditate. They need to stock up on calmness before entering the fray, and they do that through meditation.

Wavelength

Are we on the other person's wavelength? By that, I mean are we communicating in the right "channels" to suit their preferences? Have we understood whether they are primarily visual (images), auditory (sounds), or kinaesthetic (touch and feeling) in their thinking and communicating style? We're all a mixture of these, of course, but some people quite strongly favour one channel, and if our unconscious choice is distinctly different from the person we are with at the time, then we will be mismatched and struggle to communicate effectively. We will literally be speaking a different language.

If, on the other hand, we tune in to their communication preferences, we can talk to them in the same mode as they talk to themselves, and nothing is more effective than that.

To succeed in adapting to others, having an idea of our own preferences is a good start, and of course, we need to figure out those of the person to whom we want to relate. We can do this in a remarkable number of ways, too many to go into here, but the simplest is just to notice which channel they take us into when they communicate with us: visual, auditory, or kinaesthetic? Are we more aware of pictures, sounds, or feelings?

Then…

With an awareness of our own habitual preference for visual, auditory, or kinaesthetic thinking and communicating, and an ability to discern others' preferences, we can adapt what we do and say in the moment to suit those we talk to by using more visual language and materials with people who have a visual preference, and so on.

To encompass the range of different preferences

found in a group of people, we can find ways of using all three channels. One way of doing this is to illustrate a point by standing up and moving around the floor in a geometric illustration of our message.

Like many things…

Getting on the right wavelength is not an exact science, but our preferences in this area both have a very significant impact on our lives and are reflected in other aspects of our being, such as our build and the way we breathe. This is a much bigger factor in our daily experience than most people realise.

Filters

What we choose to focus on (or filter for) is a second potential area of mismatch between one individual and another. Again, it's one in which ignorance of either the principle itself or the specifics of another individual's preferences can lead to a frustrating and unsuccessful attempt to relate to that person. Our choices of what to focus on are largely unconscious, and so we are typically quite unaware of them until we do a bit of work to get to know our own preferences and develop an ability to discern the preferences of others.

Here, we are partly in the domain of the Myers-Briggs assessment and other psychometric tools. Such profiling has its place, but there are two significant drawbacks: First, you can't use it in everyday situations; and second, it can have a pigeonholing effect on the people you apply it to. They then have the opportunity to protest that they can't help their behaviour because they're a such-and-such. For that reason, profiling can actually strengthen existing patterns and reinforce an issue you are hoping to eliminate in a team, as an example.

Developing flexibility is a much better approach. Indeed, highly successful people tend to have quite balanced psychometric profiles.

We can develop an ability to discern others' filtering patterns directly and to increase our awareness of our own and adjust our behaviour accordingly. Many different filtering patterns can be identified. Here, we will cover only a few for illustration. Some of them have particular names for the character traits roles involved, indicated in brackets…

Internal or external referencing (Introvert/ Extrovert)

Some people prefer to make up their own minds. Others are very much guided by others' opinions. Some are a mixture. You can find out about this conversationally just by asking people whether they prefer to seek others' views or to make up their own mind, or a bit of both. Their preference may be context-dependent, though, so bear that in mind.

Necessity or possibility (Judger/Perceiver)

Rules guide some people's behaviour. Judgers want

to know what the structure is within which they are supposed to fit. Perceivers dislike such constraint and look for possibility instead. One way to explore this filter is to ask someone whether they would prefer to work on something where the process is all laid out and they have clear instructions to follow or whether they would be happy just to have a briefing on the overall objective and be free to develop their own way of achieving it.

Big picture or details

Some like to work at the big picture level; others need to see the details. Again, we can ask suitable questions to form an impression of someone's preferences, such as: "If we were going on a journey together, would you prefer just to know the plan for the trip as a whole or would you like to know the specific details of how we get to each destination?"

Working with filters

These three examples illustrate how different individuals make different unconscious choices about what to focus on. We need to know about these, and not just the three I've highlighted, because they determine how people respond to their circumstances.

With a little ingenuity, we can incorporate suitable questions into our normal conversation to discern where a person tends to direct his focus unconsciously. We then have the means of adapting to his preferences, if that's appropriate.

The large number of distinct filtering patterns means that the possible permutations in an individual are very large. At this level, people are remarkably different, which is a good reason for finding ways to relate to people at a more profound and universal level, so that personality differences become of secondary importance.

Connection

We all tend to connect more easily with people we perceive to be like ourselves. That may not always be the most enriching choice for us, in fact, but this like-attracting-like principle is the normal pattern. So it helps smooth the way if we find similarity with people, looking for a deep and profound connection in areas of mutual interest and concern. Minor irritations then lose their significance.

With body language—sometimes a controversial subject—take care not to be mismatched, at the very least, and be open to taking the lead from the other person in terms of how you're physically present with her. If she's animated, for example, be animated; if she's relaxed, be relaxed, and so on. Much of our communication is both non-verbal and unconscious—and, therefore, happening anyway, whether we pay attention to it or not.

Values

Know what matters. Values drive everything. People act on what they see as important. If someone's behaviour doesn't seem to make sense—if it seems "irrational"—that means we don't understand her values properly.

So we need to be skilled at finding out what a person's values are. Actually, it's pretty easy: just ask something straightforward like, "What's important to you about…?" People talk about what's important to them anyway, so all we're doing is leading them a little deeper. Of course, there's an art to doing this well. So practice, and be ready for when you need the skill. Generally, it's best to ask the question twice, because then we get a "second wave" of more deeply held, unconscious values. These are usually the ones that matter the most.

Values are a kind of guide to a person. We can use our insight to relate to them effectively and easily. Pay attention to what's important to people, and they'll help us get what we want. Clarity about all this is the basis of successful deal-making, whether explicit or implicit. It's also the basis of sustainable behaviour change.

What values determine your behaviour? Have you thought about it thoroughly? Remember you need to get to the second wave.

Language

Language is revealing if we know what to look for. Fortunately, there is a systematic approach we can adopt.

What we say and write reveals all kinds of things about not just what we're thinking, but how we're thinking about what we're thinking. In the structural form of our language is encoded all manner of clues about what is holding us back, what our true desires are, what we're muddled about, and much more—our self-imposed limitations, in other words. Alfred Korzybski started this off with his writing about "neuro-linguistics" and "general semantics" in 1933.

If you're thinking this subject sounds quite technical, you'd be right, but it's also very powerful. We can spot the linguistic features in what people say—or what we say ourselves—which highlight chances to add something to their or our thinking. The neat thing is, we can always find something to work with in what people say. When it comes to facilitating change, this really helps.

You see…

Our thinking tends to be off-kilter at times, because we approximate—brilliantly so. Most of the time, that ability serves us very well. Our senses offer up much more information than we can consciously process, so we throw most of it away. We keep only what we're looking for. If we're looking for the right thing, that's very efficient. Over time, we discard most of the information we encounter and develop a system of approximations that underpins the practical rules by which we run our lives—successfully, most of the time.

In particular, we delete, generalise, and distort information to make it fit our existing understanding. Sometimes, but only sometimes, we modify our unconsciously held model when we receive new information. This is, in many ways, a very elegant process, but it sometimes lets us down, particularly in times of change. These deletions, generalisations, and distortions show up as characteristic features in our language, which we can learn to spot—and work with too, if circumstances are conducive.

As just one example, "nominalisation" is a linguistic term for a verbal phrase turned into a noun—an abstract noun. Grammatically, this is perfectly reasonable, but the problem is much of the meaning is lost, as is the feeling of action conveyed by the original verb. Examples are "management," "empowerment," and "negotiation." (The worst offenders tend to end in "-tion" or "-ment.") To improve matters, look out for these words and turn them back into phrases with verbs. You'll find that your spoken or written word is much more compelling and clear. "Change management" is a particularly meaningless term involving a nominalisation. That's why the phrase is of so little use. "Enabling an organisation to adapt" would be an example of one better alternative, or simply "leading change."

These language patterns have a very powerful effect, and by unblocking the problems they signpost, you can be highly effective.

Self-awareness

Increasing our self-awareness is key to improving our ability to relate well to other people.

And yet…

It's surprising how many of us have very little awareness of how we come across.

We can work on our self-awareness rather easily. One way is by making use of the principle that if we change our physical state, we change our mental state. Another way is to realise that our unconscious mind doesn't really distinguish between ourselves and other people. If we imagine a conversation with another person, visualising them present and then move to their position—their chair or whatever—and look back and visualise ourselves in the chair we've just come from, we can gain remarkable insights. We can note what we like about how we are coming across and might chose to do more of, as well as what we're not so keen on and might decide to reduce or eliminate. Similarly, taking the position of an imaginary observer can be very revealing.

Attention to yourself

We need to pay attention to what we want ourselves, of course. Sometimes, it's not so easy to know what we want, but that's what we must do to be effective with other people. They need that clarity to relate effectively to us. If we know what we want, then other people will tend to help us get that, whatever it is, subject to their ability to assist us without a major impact on themselves.

First, though…

We need to be clear to ourselves about what we want, and that revolves around establishing short-term desires that are consistent with what we hope to achieve in the longer term—our vision and purpose, in fact.

Balance

To relate successfully to other people, we must achieve a balance with them, attending to what's important for them at least as much as expecting them to recognise what's important for us. That's true even if we are in a position of authority. If we take our employees' needs seriously and treat them respectfully, for example, they are much more likely to follow our lead.

At the same time, we need balance within ourselves. We need to resolve our inner tensions to present ourselves with sufficient clarity that it is possible for other people to relate to us.

We'll return to the central subject of balance shortly.

Love

We've covered this already...

Love—or if you prefer, care—makes the critical difference.

Techniques are great. Methods are great. Models are great. What really makes it all work is caring. I learned this truth in developing a systematic approach to relationship skills. (It's curious how the deeper side of a subject strengthens in response as we focus on the structure of the shallower layers.) That took me by surprise at the time.

"Care" doesn't go quite far enough. Love, in its true meaning, is the key to understanding successful human interaction everywhere. The ancients understood this, though with our modern sophistication, we might have forgotten. All the practical skills for relating to people are very useful, but without genuine human connection, something is profoundly missing. In fact, the most powerful thing is missing.

So that's it...

Love is the twelfth of twelve elements.

The benefit of a system

That then is an overview of the formula set out in *Relationship Mastery*, which, of course, I hope you will "read, learn, and inwardly digest," as my geography teacher used to say. Command of each of these skill areas provides a tremendous advantage in dealing with other people, one to be used with responsibility and integrity.

Now…

I came to the organisational learning perspective set out in the previous chapter after developing the relationship mastery formula, as I wanted to stimulate its adoption in organisations. In fact, there is a symbiotic connection: Relationship mastery helps organisational learning in general by overcoming defensive reasoning and resistance to learning, while the principles of organisational learning help impart this particular expertise in dealing with people skilfully.

I use everyday words for the twelve elements, which risks giving the impression they're just common sense. Each of these is a whole practice in itself, offering considerable advantage to the adept practitioner. Working on the twelve will make a big difference to your results. Ignore any one of them, and you risk having problems with people and not knowing why.

Of course…

You're already good at relating to people. The thing is, you could be a whole lot better, as could we all.

Relationships are fundamental.

Learn to handle them masterfully.

9

Head and Heart

Finding your Self, the ultimate resource

Too few of us are capable of employing power with love.
More of us need to learn.

— Adam Kahane

Many organisations require their people to leave their humanity at the door. That's a mistake, especially if the organisation is to adapt to change and respond to opportunities. Without humanity, there's no trust, and without trust, not much change can happen.

Increasing maturity in life involves becoming less head-centred and more heart-centred, and yet many workplaces and professions tend unwittingly to push in the opposite direction—from heart to head—trying to turn everything into numbers and processes. The snappy-sounding, but dangerous mantra phrases—"What gets measured, gets done" and "If you can't measure it, you can't manage it" (which Deming called "a costly myth")—both ignore genuine leadership and self-motivation.

We do need measures to understand the system we are dealing with—just don't expect measures or targets to be the be-all and end-all. If we're not careful, the targets become the customer, and we fall into the trap of hitting the target, but missing the point.

We have this belief that being professional means

being what we might call "head-centric" and dealing exclusively with "head stuff"—thinking and facts and figures. The problem is head stuff is inherently lacking in potential to connect with people. So it doesn't have much to contribute to leadership.

Nelson Mandela took the trouble to learn Afrikaans so that he could address the members of the white community in their mother tongue and so speak to their hearts. He believed that if we address people in what for them is a second language, they are obliged to go into their heads to understand us. They have to think and, so their response will be "head-felt" rather than heart-felt. They will disengage from an emotional connection. The ending of Apartheid in South Africa would suggest Mandela was right.

Part of the head-to-heart journey is reconnecting with our direct sensory experience—what we see, hear, and feel—which we've typically been conditioned out of expressing. In fact, by heart-centred, we really mean whole-body-centred—experiencing life not just with our heads, but also with all of us. Sometimes, that's uncomfortable, but it's real and authentic and brings us to presence.

Moving from head to heart is equivalent to a shift from ego-domination to Self-actualisation.

Signs of ego

How do you react to others' successes?

You celebrate them, of course.

Or do you? If you're like me, there's sometimes a twinge of envy—a brief moment of wishing for a similar success to report. That's not the way of mastery, however. Another's success is an enabler, a contribution to the greater good, and no threat at all, in reality—only to our ego.

If you're working towards a vision, here's a useful test of your motives and purpose: Were the goal to be achieved without you, would you welcome that, or is it more important to you to be nobly striving for success? Which matters to you more—working on change, or seeing the change happen? That's worth a moment's reflection.

And…

Would you welcome a solution to the problem you spend your working days on?

Yes, of course you would, you say. Well, let's see…

If someone turned up with news that the problem had been completely solved by other means and no further contribution was required, would you experience a sense of loss and feel that your purpose had been taken away, or be delighted that something in the world has improved? Would you immediately move on to apply your talents to another problem, however difficult and lengthy that transition might be and however much investment you have made in solving the original problem?

Chances are, the thought of the problem being solved triggers a feeling of envy or loss or both, even if only for a moment.

With that attitude, you're partly blocking a solution because your energy is pushing it away. You need the problem to remain unsolved to sustain the dissonance that motivates you to act. Not until you can welcome the solving of the problem unreservedly, no matter where the solution comes from, are you truly open to progress.

And think about this…

When you have a problem you really do want solved, take great care involving people who define themselves by that kind of work. Unconsciously, they may not really want your problem completely solved. They'll say they do, of course, but do they actually have the maturity?

Moving from ego to Self means welcoming others' successes and letting go of problems.

Power and love

As Adam Kahane makes clear in his book *Power and Love*, drawing on his experiences in South Africa and elsewhere, both head- and heart-centred approaches are required in complement with each other. Without a balance, we end up in one extreme or the other: rampant inequality or structure-less impotence.

It occurred to me that balancing power and love is the essence of the "Nelson Touch," a phrase referring to the commander of British naval forces at the Battle of Trafalgar, Admiral Horatio Lord Nelson. A little investigation confirmed this idea was exactly right.

Let's go back to 1805 and a celebrated event in British history and reflect on the crucial importance of a particular philosophy of leadership...

In explaining the nature of a man who was, even before Trafalgar, a national hero, Andrew Lambert writes that Nelson's "leadership was so much more effective than that of his fellow officers because he understood the human condition, and based his command on love, not authority. To work with Nelson was to love him: Even the most hard-bitten veterans were unable to resist his courage, commitment, and charisma. His colleagues were his friends, and he expected their love and loyalty, not mere service. He did his duty where lesser men just followed orders. This was why he earned the love of a nation. These were fine qualities on their own—when combined with an unequalled mastery of war, strategy, and politics, they changed the history of the world."

Nelson was a complex man. He had a desire to be noticed, both by his superiors and the general public, and he undoubtedly enjoyed the limelight. We might nowadays say that he was good at "public relations," and he took the art very seriously.

It seems that Nelson aspired to be like the central

character in Shakespeare's *Henry V.* Roy and Lesley Adkins note that he often spoke of himself and his captains as a "band of brothers" and "we happy few," both references to the play, in which Shakespeare portrays the King as someone who was loved by, and an inspiration to, his men.

Creating trust amongst his officers was crucial to Nelson: "By meeting with his captains and allowing them to become acquainted, he provided the conditions for them to understand and have confidence in one another. It was his genius for leadership, later known as the 'Nelson Touch,' that allowed him to rely on the simplest of strategies, instead of complicated battle plans and detailed instructions, confident that his subordinates had the ability to carry out his wishes, act independently, improvise where necessary, and support one another as a team."

That is the key point.

Nelson believed in balancing top-down leadership and bottom-up initiative. He was also both demanding and caring. He believed in leading from the front and being seen to lead from the front, accepting the considerable personal danger involved.

On the 20th of October 1805, during the Napoleonic Wars, the combined French and Spanish fleets had left Cadiz, where they'd been stationed pending an invasion of Britain. They were spotted by patrolling British frigates northwest of Cape Trafalgar. The British fleet under Nelson was waiting for the chance to bring them to battle and eliminate the threat of invasion.

At four o'clock in the morning of 21 October, Nelson ordered his ships to turn towards the enemy fleet and prepare for battle. He then went below and made a last testament asking for those dear to him to be looked after—specifically Lady Emma Hamilton and their daughter, Horatia—before returning to the quarterdeck to do his rounds and speak to members of *Victory*'s crew. Despite having 27 ships to the French Admiral Villeneuve's 33, Nelson was confident of success, because of his ships' superior fighting readiness, declaring that he would not be satisfied with taking fewer than 20 prizes. He returned briefly to his cabin to set down a prayer he had composed, after which, as Christopher Hibbert records, he joined *Victory*'s signal lieutenant John Pasco, saying...

"'Mr Pasco, I wish to say to the fleet: "England confides that every man will do his duty." You must be quick, for I have one more signal to make, which is for close action.'" (At the time, "England" was widely used to refer to the United Kingdom. In fact, 30 per cent of *Victory*'s crew and 5 of the 27 Captains in the fleet were Scots.) "Confides" meant "is confident" or "trusts."

"Pasco, having regard to the fact that the word 'confides' was not in the Signal Book and would have to be hoisted letter by letter, asked if he might substitute 'expects' which could be signalled by a single flag. 'That will do,' Nelson told him. 'Make it directly.'"

As the fleets converged, the *Victory*'s captain,

Thomas Hardy, voiced a concern that had been exercising the officers on board and suggested that Nelson remove the decorations on his coat, so that he would not be so easily identified by enemy sharpshooters. "It was too late now, Nelson said, 'to be shifting a coat.' Besides, they were 'military orders, and he did not fear to show them to the enemy.'" Captain Henry Blackwood, of the frigate HMS *Euryalus*, suggested Nelson come aboard his ship to observe the battle more clearly (and more safely). Nelson refused, and also turned down Hardy's suggestion to let Eliab Harvey's HMS *Temeraire* come ahead of the *Victory* and lead the line into battle.

Just picture the scene…

Imagine being an officer on one of the other ships of the line, for example, seeing the signal hoisted from the *Victory* heading right into the thick of it, knowing that Nelson has turned down all suggestions of avoiding personal danger. And they see the signal hoisted and decipher it…

"England expects that every man will do his duty."

The outcome, of course, is a great and decisive victory, at the cost of Nelson's own life at the age of 47, shot by a marksman from a range of 50 feet.

Pasco's change to Nelson's signal seems to shift the emphasis from an expression of belief to a statement of expectation, resulting in a more compelling, if not directing, tone. That somehow appeals to us. History perhaps must record its leaders as being more demanding—more heroic even—and less compassionate than they actually were. In fact, all in the fleet understood that what the signal really meant was that he, Nelson, was saying that he *knew* they would do their duty. They also had no doubt that he would be doing his.

Although discipline in the navy was harsh and the crews had no choice but to fight, the fact they knew Nelson cared made a great difference. They followed his leadership because he balanced both power and love.

Meanwhile, the French had effectively destroyed their navy through an excess of revolutionary zeal and unthinking top-down control. The end result was that, at Trafalgar, the British crews were, to use a modern phrase, "present in consciousness with each other," acting as a team, and the French were not. That made the difference between life and death on the day, and between success and failure. Nelson's simple strategies and his subordinates' initiative and trust in each other were decisive.

Simple, clear purpose and principles give rise to complex intelligent behaviour. Complex rules and regulations give rise to simple and stupid behaviour.

—Dee Hock

Resolving conflict

Clearly, we would hope to resolve our issues

without resorting to naval warfare, even if we were wise to retain that kind of option. The combination of resolution on the one hand and generosity on the other may succeed.

We have to take a lead in being generous, though—no use waiting for the other side. As Martin Aronson said: We may need to "dare to be gentle in a hostile world and see what fruit may come of it."

With our sense of identity seated in our Self rather than our ego, we have the strength to choose what seems like the risk of giving. This is the opposite of being defensive and is crucial to leading in challenging situations. This is not to be weak; rather it is to be strong, but in a particular way. We might ponder a line from *A Course in Miracles*: "The only thing missing from any situation is what you're not giving." In other words, only we can act.

Someone must risk returning injury with kindness,
or hostility will never turn to goodwill.

— From the *Tao Te Ching*, 79th Verse

Power and love in combination are the hallmark of a strong leader.

10

Profit and Prosperity

Reconciling egoism and altruism

No society can surely be flourishing and happy, of which the far greater part of the members are poor and miserable.

— Adam Smith

Fellowship with the human race is all very well, but how do we strike the balance between personal profit and wider prosperity?

To be fully effective in leadership roles and in stimulating change, we need clarity in our answer to this question, or we will create confusion around us. We need to decide how our leadership fits with two of the major pressures in our lives: the common good and our own private interest. How do we play our part in a society based on a balance between individual rights and social responsibilities? Moreover, how should we help craft that balance?

Putting it more crudely: If we work for the common good, how do we pay the mortgage? Or if we focus on individual gain, how do we balance that with public prosperity?

In short…

How do we balance egoism and altruism, or individualism and collectivism?

It seems to be the dilemma of the ages: how to achieve both prosperity and equality, and how to balance individual reward and collective progress? Since the beginning of time, the "haves" and the "have-nots" have been engaged in an ever-present struggle to achieve some kind of justice between them.

Traditionally, civilisation reconciled these things at the larger scale—or tried to—but the results have rarely been wholly satisfactory. Now, the onus is rather more on the individual to achieve an appropriate equilibrium, required not so much by the established systems of society, as by humanity as a whole and by the planet, because we have gone beyond the sustainable.

Some of us serve masters for whom the goal is singular and quite clear: financial profit. Others are required to deliver public good without compromise. Many, though, are at some liberty to make an individual choice between individual reward and contribution to the greater good. Are you? If so, how are you choosing to reconcile these conflicting considerations?

The ideal might seem to be equality for all, but it's not as simple as that. Ayn Rand argues in *Atlas Shrugged* that if those who contribute more are not more highly rewarded, then eventually civilisation falls apart because there is no motivation to seek progress or to contribute leadership. There is some truth in that, I believe.

Where I differ, and I suspect you may also, is that she disregards, or seems to disregard, any balancing social conscience. Indeed, she has no place for it. In my case, as a father of a son with special needs who is likely to require at least some support from society for his lifetime, how could I accept a philosophy that ignores, or even just seems to ignore, those who cannot help themselves?

Ayn Rand makes a vital point—the necessity of greater reward for greater contribution—but her belief that individuals should seek their own gain at all times is mistaken, in my view, because it fails to recognise the collective responsibilities of communities on which individual gain depends. There is no mention of raising children in *Atlas Shrugged* at all and that, I believe, gives the game away. Her thesis is an incomplete prescription—only one half of a balanced "two-legged" walk.

This is a trap we all fall into from time to time…

We argue, probably convincingly, for an alternative to the *status quo* because of its undoubted drawbacks, not realising that we still need positive features of that given norm, because we take for granted familiar, ever-present benefits that are outside conscious awareness. Such blindness is a danger when we embark on the advocacy of change. I'm vulnerable to this danger too. For example, I quote sources that support the point I believe is important, in a kind of confirmation bias. If we find ourselves championing a viewpoint, we might ask ourselves: "Were this to be a two-legged walk that I have half of, what would the other half be?"

Private interest and public good must be balanced somehow, and it is an understatement to suggest we don't always get that right as a society. Where I think we go further awry is in clinging to older ways of organising economic systems, arguing that they are the best we have, when perhaps we could make an alternative choice. We could recognise that we have the power to design something new and more suited to our times. We have been creative like that in the past, after all.

Corporation and community

Some say that community is the answer to intractable problems of the present day, but that's not wholly right either (though it may often be the missing piece). Community is not the whole answer because many of the things we rely on in everyday life depend on the actions of corporate organisations and need some hierarchical structure. For example, electrical power generation and distribution, food production, transport systems, and health care would be impossible to organise without structure. Community alone is just one part of what is needed.

If we focus solely on the community aspect, the business-minded will rightly dismiss us as irrelevant to their issues. We do need some hierarchy. The trouble starts when hierarchy becomes an end in itself. If we take a corporate approach without building a community, we will fail to harness the power of the group. To make a difference, we have no alternative but to work where these worlds of corporation and community meet.

Are you running a business, leading a movement, or championing a philosophy? It's important to be clear; otherwise, both you and the people around you will become confused, which will interfere with success. If the answer is a mixture, you need to separate each part enough to have adequate clarity.

Wealth and humanity

Adam Smith, a fellow Scot, is often cited (usually in ignorance) as being all for the unbridled capitalism of the free market through his use of the phrase "the invisible hand." As James Buchan points out in his biography of Smith, that's just not accurate. He writes: "The phrase 'invisible hand' occurs three times in the million-odd words of Adam Smith that have come down to us, and on not one of those occasions does it have anything to do with free-market capitalism." On the first occasion, "the invisible hand is not a commercial mechanism, but a circumlocution for God;" on the second, the invisible hand "is like the Great Superintendent," urging a fair distribution to all; and on the third, the invisible hand causes the merchant to improve his local economy through the rational action of furthering his own business in the geography he knows and can watch over.

Adam Smith's best-known book *An Inquiry into the Nature and Causes of the Wealth of Nations*, which dates from 1776 (the year, not entirely coincidentally, of the American Declaration of Independence), is bracketed in time by earlier and later editions of his other great work *The Theory of Moral Sentiments*. He produced seven editions of *The Theory* in all, the first one in 1759 and the last one in 1790, shortly before the end of his life. Even he covered the subjects of wealth and humanity separately, but he clearly believed in a balanced approach. Indeed he devoted his life to a holistic view.

Smith approved of what he saw emerging on the other side of the Atlantic. As James Buchan puts it, "With a clairvoyance remarkable for the year 1776, Smith saw what was to become the United States far eclipsing the mother country in trade and power." We can only speculate as to how he would judge the present and our faithfulness to the principles he admired.

Scarcity or abundance?

Whether to be a warrior or a statesperson, to use Carl Jung's framework, comes down to a choice between whether we believe in scarcity or in abundance. It's so easy to drop into worrying about payroll or paying the mortgage, but if we act in fear of scarcity, we're liable to block the flow of energy and money. If we come from a place of lack, that's what we'll attract—more lack.

The warrior stage is associated with ego-dominance, whereas the statesperson stage is associated with the Self. In the warrior mode, we're disconnected energetically from each other. From the statesperson perspective, out-and-out warrior behaviour looks rather ridiculous—and pointless. You can't take it with you, after all—material wealth, that is.

To put this in everyday terms: Are you fighting for

a share of the cake or are you working on making the cake bigger?

Abraham Maslow said that Self-actualising people—those who have moved beyond ego—are characterised by three things. First, they are independent of the good opinion of other people, meaning they do what they believe is right. Second, they are detached from the outcome. The result they get is just something to be learned from, not something to get emotional about one way or the other. And third, they are not invested in power over other people. They may have authority, but they don't enjoy it for its own sake. Self-actualisers believe in abundance.

There's a difference between power to do something and power over other people. If we have power to do something, particularly if we are invested with that kind of authority, we have a duty to use that power, but we don't have the right to relish power over other people. We also need to be on guard for power corrupting us. That happens so easily, and when it does, we are the losers.

Egoism and altruism

In recent times, we've built up the culture of the hero leader and a method of running organisations based on egoism and "power over." The result is a very top-down approach.

To make progress, we need to let go of this need for

complete control. Too much control and no one can change. Other people need some room to move. We may need to accept a balance of chaos and order. Often, though, as Dee Hock says, people are "trapped by the same old paradigms of predictability and control. They want to know how things will end before they begin. They don't want to create the conditions for solutions to emerge without being able to control what those solutions might be."

Even if you're the most capable person in the organisation or the situation, you're still only the most capable person. That's much less capable than the group as whole can be, and to collaborate, you need to be prepared to share power. If you're not sharing power, it's not collaboration.

At the same time, paradoxically, we've established a belief that teams and groups will always come up with better results than individuals; that the collective is always better than the individual. Actually, history doesn't back this up, as Susan Cain demonstrates in her book *Quiet*. Most big breakthroughs and creative masterpieces have been made by people working, or at least thinking, largely on their own—Einstein, for example. To excel, we may need to resist the urge to belong and instead be content in our own company—in both senses of the word.

We have a balance to strike between acting alone and acting together. We need to decide whether a collective effort or individual creativity is the right choice at any particular time. We need both altruism and egoism—and a balance between them.

We all have a fear of insignificance, driven by our ego. Of course, in most respects, we are insignificant, in global terms. Oddly enough, when we accept that, we might start to have influence.

Structural conflict and the importance of choice

Egoism versus altruism could be seen as an example of "structural conflict"—two or more feedback loops in which the means of resolution are mutually exclusive. In this case, insecurity may drive actions in pursuit of personal reward. These actions then likely create consequences that fuel unease about our relative good fortune and lack of contribution to the greater good, at which point we become more altruistic and tend to neglect our own needs, until feelings of insecurity return and the cycle begins again, as indicated below...

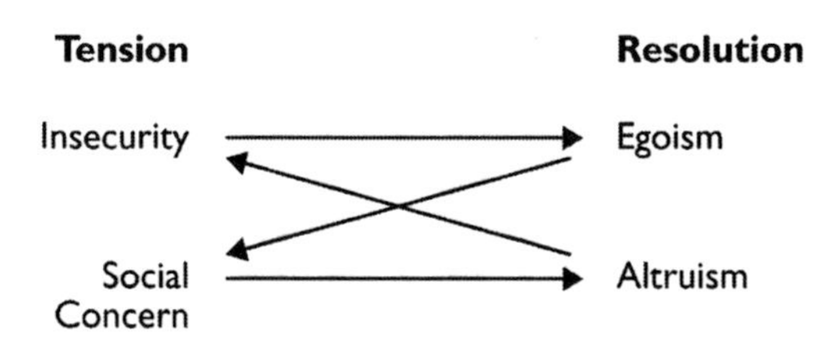

Structural conflict, as it stands, is not resolvable: We just have to choose a point of balance. Problems come from trying to make the issue go away. It won't. The end result of trying is likely to see us oscillating between one extreme and the other, and a feeling of emotional tension. Both individuals and organisations can oscillate in this way. The cost can be significant, physically and mentally. We need to make choices and learn to respect them, living them in full. That way, we at least have a consistency. Don't expect everyone around you necessarily to like your choice, but if you respect your own choices, they will too. Do change them if you need to, though. On the face of it, balance between egoism and altruism is something about which we must reach our own conclusions.

On the other hand, if we change our beliefs about the structure of the issue, we may change our experience of it. What do we get when we blend egoism and altruism—something different entirely? We will revisit this question shortly.

Private interest or public good?

I have found profit and prosperity a difficult subject to address because my own thinking has not been clear, nor has my action. However, as is often the way, my outlook changed in the course of writing. Now I see the issue of egoism and altruism anew, and have made a different choice.

I recalled a marketing expert, Ted Nicholas, saying that if we can't sell something, we probably won't be able to give it away either. I'd thought of that as applying mostly to physical products, but it occurred to me that it applied to services and ideas too. So there's not much point in championing ideas out of altruism. If we can't find someone who values what we have to offer highly enough to pay us something for it, then we probably won't succeed in giving the ideas away either. So we might as well take a commercial approach and look for genuine "customer pull."

As a consequence, I've become a little less altruistic and a little more commercial in drawing this chapter together. I've also withdrawn from some non-profit activities that I decided weren't helping me and that I wasn't helping. Without some personal reward, we can't keep serving the public good.

"Put on your own oxygen mask before helping others," and all that.

Egoism and altruism in organisations

So it's a question of balance: an excess of altruism, and an organisation may become unviable; an excess of egoism, and it may become dysfunctional in another way.

As Ian Cunningham writes, "All the evidence is that egocentric leadership models... are damaging to organisations and to people." He goes on, "We will never solve the range of social problems that many countries such as the UK and USA face unless gross inequalities are reduced."

Some companies forget that their primary purpose is to serve their customers and thereby make a return.

Instead, they behave as if their customers exist in service of their profits. They'll deny that, of course, but judge for yourself. The change of emphasis is critical and usually leads to trouble in the longer term when the market decides it's no longer happy to be treated as a commodity.

So remember that an organisation exists to serve customers in some sense and, in so doing, reward its stakeholders, not the other way round. And don't be tempted by the path of the hero leader, trying to do it all yourself and controlling everything. Real leadership quietly stimulates a collective effort.

Effective leaders balance egoism and altruism. Neither dominates.

11

Answers in Balance

Handling ambiguity, finding your way

The opposite of a correct statement is an incorrect statement, but the opposite of a profound truth may well be another profound truth.

— Niels Bohr

Some of the most important questions have not one right answer, but two opposite ones—or even more than two—and yet our upbringing has ingrained within most of us the need to find the perfect response. We feel compelled to pursue the search for that single right answer when in fact many of these quests are futile, or even damaging.

The reality is…

On many issues, two considerations (like egoism and altruism) sit in opposition and must be held in balance if a sustainable solution is to be found. This can be challenging. As F. Scott Fitzgerald said, "The test of a first-rate intelligence is the ability to hold two opposed ideas in the mind at the same time and still retain the ability to function." So, single-mindedness isn't necessarily a desirable trait, at least not all the time. Rather, "double-mindedness" could be a mark of wisdom.

Deeper questions, especially, may have a pair of answers—two of Niels Bohr's profound truths. Accepting that we live in a world of duality and appreciating the implications is highly liberating. Our search for the one right answer can cease. It's futile—simply pointless. Yet that's the Holy Grail we are liable to end up pursuing if we are not careful.

Many want the apparent simplicity of a single "right" answer. As a result, they invest a great deal of effort in debate, trying to establish who's right and who's wrong, when the reality is both are. What a waste of time, and yet we see this played out routinely in public discourse, with attempts to decide the winner of an argument—ridiculous when we could know at the outset that both are correct. Often, we're actually weighing the ability to argue or simply dominate rather than the underlying merit of the case.

Instead…

The profitable question to address is how to balance the opposing considerations. If we duck that challenge and instead pick one alternative, we can be sure that we'll eventually have to come round to the other choice. The adverse consequences of our first departure from the balanced path will eventually become overwhelming, and we'll have to change course.

The first step, though, is adjusting to the absence of a single answer to many questions. Life isn't as simple as we might have expected it to be.

Or perhaps it's simpler: We just need to look at it another way.

Both… and…

We may find it disorientating to recognise that some questions—profound ones, especially—have not one right answer but two opposite ones, which we then need to reconcile. That may be a disconcerting realisation, but also a profound relief. In fact, balance is at the heart of many issues. Often, we need both one thing and another thing; we need both… and… We need a "two-legged walk." A one-legged walk—otherwise known as hopping, of course—isn't that effective a means of proceeding.

Duality is everywhere in nature. For example, as mentioned already, some scientific observations can only be understood if electrons can behave like both particles and waves, depending on circumstances.

To bring ourselves into balance, we must first become clear about what the contradictory elements are. What is the ambiguity, exactly? In fact, there are many pairs of these, some of which are already familiar. Here's a list of sorts:

Standing out and fitting in
Task and relationship
Power and love
Top-down and bottom-up
Chaos and order
Knowing and not knowing
Leading and following
Masculine and feminine

Capitalism and social justice
Warrior and statesperson
Competition and cooperation
Conscious and unconscious
Matter and energy
Head and heart
East and West
Ancient and modern
Scarcity and abundance
Complexity and simplicity
Prosperity and equality
Objective and subjective
Ego and Self
Tangible and intangible
Division and wholeness
Individual and collective
Thinking and doing
Egoism and altruism
Directing and supporting
Yin and Yang
Management and leadership
Change and stability

Merely finding a point of permanent compromise between extremes is unlikely to be successful, especially if we hope to influence others. Instead, we must learn that balance is dynamic in nature, with an ebb and flow between one consideration and its alternate. Without that flexibility, we are unlikely to make sufficient connection with those we seek to influence. Unless we acknowledge and respect their point of view, they won't accept ours.

So...

We need to encompass all the valid perspectives on an issue to which there is no single right answer. The ability to lead change comes from the grace and ease with which we respect any one consideration to build a relationship with people—and then introduce another perspective to influence them in the direction we believe is useful. We are, therefore, in the business of balancing equally valid but apparently inconsistent or even irreconcilable factors. As Claudia Madrazo and Peter Senge write, "We have seen that many of the most effective system change leaders are masters at holding to this 'both/and' perspective."

Balance with other people matters. Balance is also important within ourselves, between the different parts of our being. Carl Jung stressed the importance of balancing opposites. Once two conflicting trends are brought into consciousness, the tension between them can be resolved. Then a new, third state representing a healthier attitude can emerge.

Masculine and feminine

How many wars can you think of that were started by a woman?

No, I can't think of many either.

In general, men and women see things differently. Accommodating these perspectives is essential, even in one individual of either gender. This is perhaps most easily expressed as the balance between the Yin (feminine) and the Yang (masculine).

In Western society, women are typically underrepresented in leadership positions, though that is slowly changing. This matters, of course, for equality of opportunity: the frame in which the subject is usually discussed, but it also matters for a wider reason. Without the balance of male and female perspectives in leadership thinking, results will be suboptimal—the one won't have the opportunity to compensate for the other. As it says in the *Tao Te Ching*, "Know the strength of a man, but keep a woman's care!" or in Wayne Dyer's words, recognise that "female energy, or Yin, is the true receptor of all; by remaining quiet and still, it ultimately overcomes male (Yang) efforts to subjugate and conquer."

That's not to say that achieving that balance will be easy or comfortable. It's much easier for the male to exclude the female, to convene with other men, and reach decisions with apparent ease. The question, of course, is: Are these decisions the best ones?

Experience might suggest that women are more alive to the heart connection, whereas men typically are more head-centred and ego-dominated, but that's not always the case.

Finding the way

We've accepted that many questions have not one right answer but two, or maybe more than two, and therefore, we need a "both... and..." approach—a two-legged walk. What we haven't solved is how to blend the two components effectively. Sometimes, we'll be able to find a way of integrating the two extremes into a single way forward—some kind of unifying answer. Other times, it's not so simple. In some cases, we can't adopt a single alternative, or at least we don't yet know how to. And in the meantime, we need to make practical progress.

Moreover...

Some of our "both... and..." pairs aren't points at either end of a continuum. The structure isn't so linear. Take leading and following, for example: What's halfway along a line joining these two? The answer is not so obvious. Is there even a line between them, or are they completely distinct from each other?

We could switch from one alternative to the other as seems appropriate in the moment, but we may feel clumsy doing that, and we will probably come across as clumsy too. We're likely to lose influence.

Instead...

We need to break free from our Western conditioning and borrow from Taoism in earnest, specifically the idea of Yin and Yang as a complementary pair in constant ebb and flow. In the Yin-Yang symbol, each aspect contains a little of its opposite, represented by a small circle of the other colour or energy. So if we are unable to harmonise two opposites into a single blended approach, we at least have the idea of moving between them in a smooth, flowing manner. The central curving line in the symbol representing the Yin and the Yang indicates "the way" or the path between the opposites, smoothly balancing their influences.

One manifestation of this philosophy is in the practice of T'ai Chi, an Oriental discipline of movement designed to harmonise the body with itself and with the mind. T'ai Chi, significantly, is characterised by highly elegant, flowing movements.

Now...

I must acknowledge a debt to a friend, Ken Symon, who provided a particularly prescient comment when I described the dichotomy to him—how to handle two opposing but equally necessary ideas. Ken said, "In T'ai Chi, you're never double-weighted." I wasn't exactly sure what he meant at first, but the point is: The T'ai Chi practitioner's weight is always in transition from one foot to the other, from left to right and back again as she moves, never statically on both feet, except at the beginning and end of the practice.

Ken didn't specifically mention the flowing aspect—the gradual waxing and waning between one side and another and the full significance didn't occur to me until later, but here it is: If we have to alternate between extremes such as power and love, we should do so in a flowing, smooth manner, not a discontinuous switching. That way, we can preserve our congruence and our connection with other people.

Opposite or orthogonal?

If we think of "relaxed" and "controlled" (or any other both... and... pair) as opposite points on a continuum like this (see below), then we will struggle to reconcile them effectively because we can only choose one at the expense of the other...

If, on the other hand, we see them as orthogonal, then there is no fundamental difficulty in blending both at a high pitch, such as at "x" below...

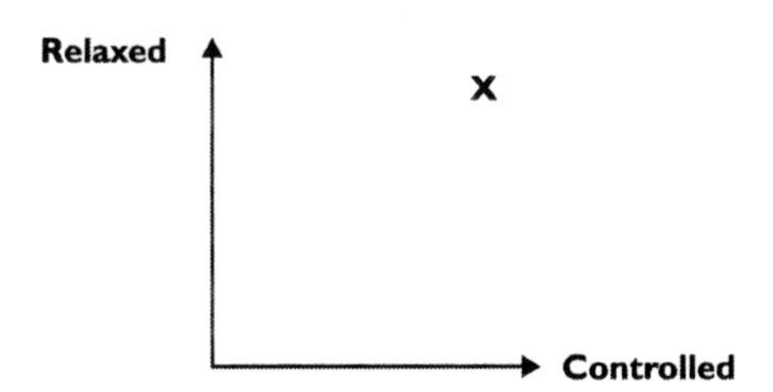

Physically, it's not possible to go East and West at the same time, but we can perfectly well travel North and East. Also, if we think, for example, of a highly proficient snowboarder, are they more relaxed or more controlled than a beginner? The answer, of course, is they are both.

Holding to both... and... is a bit like balancing a stick upright on the end of our finger: It takes constant attention to keep it there. Blending top-down and bottom-up energy in organisations should be like this—a dynamic balance between the one and the other. Unfortunately, in most organisations, the metaphorical stick fell to the ground years ago. But we can pick it up again.

Towards wholeness

In holding to a both... and... perspective, or even integrating complementary ideas, we're doing more than balancing: We're reversing, as best we can, the inevitable process of fragmentation which takes place through time. As David Bohm says, for many of our issues, if we don't bring the pieces back together, we have little hope of solving the problem simply because we don't have access to all the parts we need to blend together.

To reconcile opposing factors, we need to create first a reasonable degree of integration between them, starting at our own individual level. Holding all the considerations in our own minds is the beginning of reconciling them amongst a group of people.

We need to get our unconscious involved. Sometimes, our body knows how to balance different factors even if our conscious mind doesn't. A simple but powerful approach is to hold each of the two ideas, one in either hand, almost literally, giving each associated role a name. Realise that ultimately both lead to the same higher outcome—our inner peace, essentially. Notice what each offers the other in the way of learning.

The next step in this contemplative process is to bring our two hands together and allow our body or mind to tell us something about what the merged entity is. In doing this, we're bringing our whole being to bear on the question. Something about bringing opposing ideas together physically stimulates a realignment of our thoughts around a new central idea, or at least one that is new to our conscious awareness.

Returning to an earlier question…

Must we always choose between leading and following, or is there another alternative? Can we integrate these two?

I found I could, after a lot of effort. The answer—for me anyway—is being present, as I mentioned earlier. Now, I can't tell you that I arrived at this liberating realisation through a logical process, and that, in a way, is the point: Blending opposites requires a generative, imaginative approach.

Being present feels whole. It has a very different

energy, on a different dimension, to the two starting points: Leading and following.

Egoism and altruism—revisited

So what happens if we apply this process to the tension between private interest and public good? Here's how it is for me…

In my left hand is egoism in the person of "the provider;" in my right is altruism—"the sharer." Right away, as I work this process, I am horrified by the weight the provider carries in contrast to the lightness of the sharer. I feel it physically. My unconscious is giving me a powerful signal.

What's the higher purpose of each part? The provider wants sufficiency that will, in turn, bring profound relief and peace. The sharer's peace comes from leaving a legacy and making a difference. They want the same thing ultimately (peace). Are they willing to collaborate? Yes. The sharer can offer the provider the insight that the family will be all right. The provider suggests the sharer can afford to be more commercial, more resolute.

So I bring my hands slowly together, looking for a physical signal of new insight—at first, there's nothing. Then I realise there's something about movement. My body wants my hands to move, and I have a sense of moving liquid around. The word that fits best is "orchestrator" or perhaps even "mover and shaker." My realisation is about getting the flow going—encouraging it along, physically. What comes to me is that when the provider and the sharer work together, they become an orchestrator: So if I blend egoism and altruism, I get orchestration, which makes sense because flow creates abundance and that provides more of both individual reward and public good.

I'm pleased with that discovery, and I notice all the more reason why fear is no damn good because it shuts down the flow necessary to balance egoism and altruism.

Now…

We may not always be able to integrate completely or balance every angle of a problem. We may not be able to reverse the fragmentation and bring everything to wholeness. How we deal with that shortfall in our ability to find a middle or single way is what makes the difference. The grace with which we do that is "the difference that makes the difference," in fact.

We can't make everything whole all at once—neither every issue nor ourselves. That's a lifetime's work, but we can proceed in the right direction all the time.

When it comes to leadership, we're on a process of integration as well. Of necessity, we're addressing the whole person, not just the part that shows up for the working day or the part a family sees or the part friends see, which might all be different. In leadership, we need to deal with the whole iceberg, not just the part above the water.

Balance in organisations

Trust in the ability of other people to handle ambiguity. They'll do better with that than with inconsistency. We don't need to keep our conflict to ourselves. We can share the dilemma. Of course, we need to coach them to manage contradiction, but they are probably better equipped to cope with the uncertainties than we give them credit for. And they may even come up with innovative solutions we would never have considered.

If you doubt this…

Look at the evidence of voting in elections: A large body of people usually comes to a collective decision that is remarkably balanced with respect to all the considerations, disappointing though the outcome may be for many involved. That happens even though many in the electorate are supposedly ill-informed and easily influenced by the media. Neither of these is the case, of course, just as ordinary working people are sometimes wiser than their leaders.

Integrate the parts.

Address the whole.

Find the way.

12

Self and System

Stimulating change

We have met the enemy and he is us.

— Pogo

Influencing a wider system like an organisation or a community or even a country can happen to the extent that we are in connection with a significant number of people (i.e., we are present "in consciousness" with them and they with us), and we undertake the inner change work that we need to tackle personally. Then the people we are connected with will be influenced to change too, not necessarily in exactly the same manner as we have changed ourselves, but at least in the same direction.

I don't know how to prove this principle to you, but I can cite a prominent example: Ian Paisley was a Unionist preacher and politician in Northern Ireland, who began implacably opposed to any accommodation with the Republican side. Yet after decades, he eventually travelled a road that led both to peace and strong friendship with his principal opponent Martin McGuinness. Because he was such a hardliner to begin with and was so well known, he brought a critical mass of people with him on the journey to reconciliation as he made a courageous new choice for himself. It might have been better if he'd got there more quickly, but nevertheless.

I do know that if you act as if this principle is true, you'll find it works, and what's more, it's the only way that works. We're like a cog in a big machine: When we turn, everything else turns. Stay still, and everything else stays still.

As Claudio Madrazo and Peter Senge put it in their paper *Being the Change: Building Communities of Collaboration and Co-inspiration for Systemic Change*, "Our normal stance is to see ourselves as separate from the reality we seek to change. This limits our effectiveness in ways that can be difficult to see. We see the problem as 'out there,' and we see our job as 'change agents' as getting someone else to change. When we do this, we take no responsibility for the causes of the problem and often end up pursuing manipulative change strategies." They continue: "Alternatively, we can adopt the orientation that 'we are part of the system' and that whatever is dysfunctional in the larger system operates within us as well."

When we address the dysfunction within ourselves, we influence the system to change too.

A model of organisational change

Having in mind a structured approach to a change programme for the outer system is a good idea. John Kotter sets out a proven model of organisational change in his book *Leading Change*. I've outlined the eight-stage process here:

1. Establishing a sense of urgency

First, we need to disrupt the complacency of

remaining as we are, through articulating the realities we face or the opportunities we see. We may need to create a sense of crisis, if one doesn't exist.

2. Creating the guiding coalition

We need to bring together a group, probably a disparate one, with enough power to lead the change. We need to develop that group as a team.

3. Developing a vision and strategy

We need to create a picture of how we would like things to be and a strategy to get there. As many people as possible should be involved in the visioning process.

4. Communicating the change vision

We need to communicate the vision and strategy through every means possible and on multiple occasions. The members of the guiding coalition must model the behaviour expected of all involved.

5. Empowering broad-based action

We need to remove obstacles. These could be existing systems that support the *status quo*. We need to encourage risk-taking too.

6. Generating short-term wins

We must specifically plan for and achieve visible improvements in the near-term. We must then reward those who create these plans and achievements.

7. Consolidating gains and producing more change

We should use the short-term wins and increasing credibility that results from them to initiate more of the needed change and to hire the right people. We can bring in new projects, themes, and change agents as needed, and we should avoid declaring victory too soon.

8. Anchoring new approaches in the culture

We must highlight connections between new behaviours and organisational success so that the new way becomes the norm. Better leadership and more effective management must become prevalent.

Many of these stages fall into the easy-when-you-say-it-quickly category. In his book, John Kotter stresses, in particular, the amount of effort required for communicating the change vision, through every available channel, in every way possible, again and again. He says a common error is "under-communicating the vision by a factor of 10 (or 100 or even 1,000)." I would add that the repetition is needed (and often overlooked) because all behavioural change is unconscious.

John Kotter doesn't address at all the inner path—our individual change work as leaders. We can be much more effective when we combine the wisdom of his approach with the power of personal presence and our own example.

The outside reflecting the inside

Imagine that what's inside us is a reflection of what's outside and *vice versa*. If that's true, then change in either will be reflected in the other. That sounds a bit implausible, I suppose, but think about this…

We generally act as if we understand our world, but we don't really. We think we're solid, but we're actually mostly empty space. It's just that the way our eyes see these materials, they seem to be solid. Things aren't what they seem. Maybe the outside really is related to the inside. We could advance an argument from quantum physics as to why that could be so.

At a more prosaic level, we know that we project onto other people things we are not acknowledging about ourselves—our "shadow." What if our whole experience of the outside world is a projection? The only things we notice are things that are already inside us. (Some of the Eastern philosophies say that life is really to be experienced on the inside, not in the external sensory world we seem to inhabit.) So if we change what's inside us, we'll change what we notice outside. Then we're likely to reinforce the things we want to see, just by paying attention to them. And so the world will change—in appearance, and in reality too.

Once we understand that progress in the outer world depends on progress within, we see that something we thought was outside our control is more in our gift than we realised. We might also notice that, in fact, we're setting the pace—well, holding it back, probably.

And so we want to hurry it along. We want to push on with our own change work, but it may not happen so fast or so easily. We may need some compassion for ourselves. Change can take time.

Just do it?

To hurry the pace in an organisation, we could perhaps say: "Just do it." But seriously, have you tried that lately? Of course, be demanding if you have the authority to do so, but you're probably going to need something else. Chances are that trying to achieve change by edict isn't going to work very well, even when we apparently have authority to "make it happen." People have ways of backsliding. The change will revert when our attention is elsewhere.

We need something much more self-sustaining—more emergent—if change is going to last. We need a bottom-up effect. The way to stimulate that effect is, counter-intuitively for most of us, to look to our own inner change work and growth because that's what we will then inspire in other people. In turn, this change will grow as a bottom-up, sustainable development. As Claudia Madrazo and Peter Senge write, "Herein lies a subtlety of real systemic change: What is most systemic is most personal, and those capable of leading in such efforts truly understand this." For example, Mother Teresa became highly influential through, as she put it, "doing small things with great love." It is paradoxical... the smaller we act, it seems, the wider the effect.

Take on difficulties while they are still easy;
do great things while they are still small.
The sage does not attempt anything very big,
and thus achieves greatness.

— From the *Tao Te Ching*, 63rd Verse

Do small things well.

Then big things change.

Leading to Success

Gathering it all together

Simplicity is the ultimate sophistication.

— Leonardo da Vinci

Sustainable success—sustainable anything, in fact—requires change, especially in a more and more rapidly evolving world. And change requires leadership: not heroic, top-down leadership, but a more subtle and ultimately more effective ability to stimulate whole-hearted, intelligent participation and self-organising action by a body of people.

Our ability to be influential and effective in this way depends more than anything on the quality and strength of our presence. Leadership, therefore, begins within. That, however, is not where we usually start.

Now...

We do need skilful approaches to the outward aspect of leading organisations, to the nurturing of organisational learning as a means of making evolution self-sustaining, and to understanding the structure of successful change. Of course, we need that, but we can make bigger strides forward and make them more easily by doing a great job of leading ourselves.

Moreover...

Working on the inner side of leadership, we can make whatever changes we like. We have all the pieces, and we don't need to wait for anyone else. We may need to wait for our own increasing maturity, but even that ultimately flows from the choices we make.

To the extent we are in connection with other people when we change, we will influence them to change as well. Our relationship with the external system means change achieved inside becomes change inspired outside—provided we have the necessary presence, that is. Much of this influence is an unconscious process, which is the point most people miss, because, of course, it's unconscious.

Instead...

We're much more focused—perhaps exclusively focused—on rational, conscious thinking perspectives, which we call "professional," while we discount the intangible, the emotional and the subjective—the human dimension.

It's conventional in talking about leadership, especially in organisations, to avoid anything much to do with our common humanity and not go anywhere near questions of belief and faith and human connection (love). These are frightening things to talk about. They make us uncomfortable. So we leave them as personal matters. And so, in organisations and in society as well, we stay fragmented and stuck. That is exactly the problem.

We prefer to talk about power and direction and other masculine, Yang traits of leadership. We do need these. We absolutely do. But we need the Yin traits too. We need to bring the two into balance. To lead effectively, as Adam Kahane says, we need to be able to work with both power and love, with both the Yin and the Yang.

Faced with a challenge, most professional people go deeper into the intellectual domain with ever more complex thinking—more "head stuff." Often, a much easier and ultimately more powerful answer lies in another dimension altogether—that of our common humanity. Of course, that field is generally not seen as academically or administratively sound, and therein lies the issue: The very thing that is the solution to the problem—dealing well with the intangible—may be precluded because it's not tangible; it isn't evidential in nature; it's not professional. We can't measure it.

What a stupid way to be stuck, an illustration of what Ayn Rand called "the glaringly evident which everybody has decided not to see."

To break free…

We need to become adept at balancing the tangible and the intangible, as well as the many other pairs of complementary or even opposing factors we must learn to blend. Another is the need for top-down direction and bottom-up emergence of sustainable solutions. To many questions, there may not be one right answer. More often, we need to balance two opposite considerations. It's not a case of choosing one or the other; it's a case of blending complementary approaches. Just realising that is often a good start. Frequently, clear ambiguity is all the clarity we need. Then our ability to hold our state and the resulting strength of our presence will influence those around us.

In a world that relentlessly separates, we need to

bring the pieces back together if we are to solve the problems we face. Without all the components, we have no hope of resolving the whole.

If we care to look, we'll find that duality, balance, and integration show themselves as themes at every scale, from subatomic particles to the whole Universe and all our earth-bound endeavours in between. Science has moved on from expecting everything to be deterministic. Our organisations could do with catching up. In reality, we can't know everything, and it's time to stop pretending we do, because that delusion is inhibiting.

Sometimes, we will be able to integrate one consideration and another into a single, unified approach. Other times we won't—at least not at the time. The art is to move gracefully and gradually from one to the other. We must respect both perspectives to be effective.

On a bigger scale…

Using a structured approach, we can lead change, make organisations more self-adapting, and overcome the resistance to learning and growth that is very likely to get in the way. That resistance is everywhere, stemming, as it does, from our human nature and our immaturity, in which we are dominated by our egos.

Rather than trying to deal with such difficulties intellectually—which really is hard—we can see that resistance to change and learning arises from ego and, therefore, from fear. Ultimately, fear is an absence of love. So the answer is to build strong relationships, and we can learn to be good at that. By far the easiest way to handle the ego is to come from the heart, not the head. It's very simple: Act from the heart and most things work, come from the head and they probably won't. Teams that care outperform teams that don't.

As we develop a higher level of maturity, thinking with the heart as well as with the head and identifying more with the Self than with the ego, we become open to learning and change. So it surely makes sense for leaders of organisations to foster humanity in their people and community in their organisation, even if difficult decisions with painful consequences have to be made from time to time.

Human connection is also the way to work across "silos" in an organisation and engage successfully with the "tribes" that inhabit them. If someone is disrupting that kind of trust and confidence—and it only takes one—we must do something about it.

The interplay of ego and Self also expresses itself in the balance we must find between our private interest and the public good—between altruism and egoism. Neither is sustainable on its own.

So…

We need to rediscover our humanity and reintegrate it into what we do, including how we lead organisations in all their forms. That is the missing enabler. You may notice the power of what business and other leaders say multiplies many times over when they touch on some aspect of common humanity. And yet they often apologise for the inclusion. We have an opportunity now to make a different choice: to tap into that power deliberately. Authentic human connection is the most powerful force available and the one that makes everything else possible.

Leadership, as opposed to management, is ultimately about being adept at working with the intangible factors like love, faith, and belief, which bring so much power to situations with other people. To succeed in that, we need to let go of the need for rational explanation. Cling to it and we will be forever limited. Approaches to leadership that pass the normal tests of academic scholarship (i.e., evidence), useful though they may be, must forever fall short of a full prescription because they cannot truly embrace the whole.

Leadership depends on faith—faith in oneself, faith in others, faith in possibility, and, well, just faith. If, as Voltaire said, "Faith consists in believing when it is beyond the power of reason to believe," then it follows that leadership is beyond the power of reason. So don't try to reason it. Just be it. Belief needs to come from you. Find your strength within.

Far from being a dead end, that realisation is a new beginning. It sets us free. Just because we can't fully explain something, doesn't mean it doesn't work. Freeing ourselves from the need for tangible evidence, we can choose our own approach to leadership. We can assess for ourselves the effect of our actions and adjust accordingly. We can see the difference between fact and truth.

Then we will have presence as a leader. Success in organisations, in societies, and in life will follow.

Leadership requires personhood
and developing that
is open to everybody.

Bibliography

Adkins, Roy and Adkins, Lesley *The War for All the Oceans: From Nelson at the Nile to Napoleon at Waterloo*, Little, Brown, London, 2006
An account of the Napoleonic Wars with crucial insights into the nature of Nelson's leadership at sea.

Argyris, Chris *Teaching Smart People How to Learn*, Reprinted from *Harvard Business Review* (May 1991), Boston, 2008
Chris Argyris articulates with great clarity the propensity of organisations and individuals to be predisposed not to learn, and why this happens. This is a crucial piece, conveyed in a paper.

Argyris, Chris *Knowledge for Action: A Guide to Overcoming Barriers to Organisational Change*, Jossey-Bass, San Francisco, 1993
An expression in book form of Chris Argyris's vital contribution around anti-learning, defensive reasoning and skilled incompetence.

Aronson, Martin (editor) *Jesus and Lao Tzu: The Parallel Sayings*, Ulysses Press, Berkeley, 2000
As the title indicates, this book draws connections between Christianity and Taoism—indications perhaps of a "Perennial Philosophy," in the words of Aldous Huxley.

Benson, Nigel C. *Introducing Psychology: A Graphic Guide*, Icon Books, London, 2003
An accessible overview of the main strands of psychology, this textbook includes Maslow's work.

Bohm, David *On Dialogue*, Routledge, Abingdon, 1996
The key principles of dialogue are set out here—dialogue as opposed to discussion and debate, that is.

Bohm, David *Wholeness and the Implicate Order*, Routledge, Abingdon, 1980
David Bohm is one of many of the prominent physicists who are or were also philosophers. They addressed wider questions than just their science.

Buchan, James *Adam Smith: and the Pursuit of Perfect Liberty*, Profile Books, London, 2007
An accessible and succinct account of the man and his famous works from the 18th Century.

Cain, Susan *Quiet: The Power of Introverts in a World That Can't Stop Talking*, Penguin, London, 2012
Surprisingly perhaps, teams and extrovert leaders don't always outperform individuals.

Carnegie, Dale *How to Win Friends and Influence People* (Revised Edition), Vermilion, London, 2006
The classic book on relationships, which is just as vital today as when first published in 1937.

Cialdini, Robert B. *Influence: The Psychology of Persuasion*, HarperCollins, New York, 1984
Sets out six powerful factors of influence that can be used for good or ill. Best to be aware.

Collins, Jim *Good to Great: Why Some Companies Make the Leap... and Others Don't,* Random House, London, 2001
A study of what made the difference in what became great businesses.

Covey, Stephen R. *The 7 Habits of Highly Effective People: Powerful Lessons in Personal Change*, Simon & Schuster, London, 1989
A modern classic on making the most of one's life.

Cox, Brian and Forshaw, Jeff *The Quantum Universe: Everything That Can Happen Does Happen*, Penguin, London, 2011
Accessible treatment of quantum mechanics and its connection with astronomy.

Cunningham, Ian *Leadership development in crisis: leadership development hasn't made much difference to organisations*, Development and Learning in Organizations, Vol. 24, No. 5, 2010, pp. 5–7
Makes the case that egocentric "hero" leadership isn't a great idea, for either organisations or people.

De Geus, Arie *The Living Company*, Nicholas Brealey, London, 1999
Sets out the idea that it can be useful to consider companies as if they were organisms in their own right with a separate existence and not just as a legal entity. They change and adapt, or not, as the case may be.

Deming, W. Edwards *The New Economics: For Industry, Government, Education*, MIT Press, Cambridge, MA, 1994
Sets out Deming's principles for acting systemically.

Dyer, Wayne *Manifest Your Destiny: The Nine Spiritual Principles for Getting Everything you Want*, Element, London, 1997
One of many books from the same author making sense of spirituality and other matters. A major influence.

Dyer, Wayne *Change Your Thoughts—Change Your Life: Living the Wisdom of the Tao*, Hay House UK, London, 2007
Wayne Dyer's interpretation of the Tao Te Ching. Profoundly helpful, in my experience.

Early, Gene *3 Keys To Transforming Your Potential*, Noble News and Books, Harrisonburg, Virginia, 2014
A key influence, especially about presence.

Easwaran, Eknath (translator) *The Bhagavad Gita*, Nilgiri Press, Tomales, CA, 1985
An ancient source of wisdom, this time from India.

Einstein, Albert *Relativity: The Special & the General Theory*, Martino Publishing, Mansfield Centre, CT, 2010
Einstein's own book on Relativity for a mainstream audience. Less challenging than a full-blown scientific treatment, but still challenging.

Farrelly, Frank and Brandsma, Jeff *Provocative Therapy*, Meta Publications, Capitola, 1974
A book for therapists and those who want to stop pussyfooting around, with much to learn from Frank about effective and loving use of directness and humour.

Feynman, Richard *QED: The Strange Theory of Light and Matter*, Penguin, London, 1990
Accessible treatment on some of the mysteries of science.

Godin, Seth *Tribes: We Need You to Lead Us*, Piatkus, London, 2008
A concise articulation of why we act in groups and the consequences.

Godin, Seth *Linchpin: Are You Indispensable?* Piatkus, London, 2010
A book about choosing to make a difference.

Handy, Charles *Myself and Other More Important Matters*, Arrow, London, 2007
A wise guide in many ways.

Hibbert, Christopher *Nelson: A Personal History*, Da Capo, Boston, MA, 1994
Amongst much else, provides fine detail of Nelson's actions prior to and during his last battle.

Hock, Dee *One From Many: VISA and the Rise of Chaordic Organisation*, Berrett-Koehler, San Francisco, 2005
An authority on the both... and... principle.

Hogshead, Sally *Fascinate: Your 7 Triggers to Persuasion and Captivation*, HarperCollins, New York, 2010
Compelling—fascinating even—account of what we find fascinating and why, principally in the context of marketing, but with insights for leadership too, which of course is a kind of marketing.

Hopper, Kenneth and Hopper, William *The Puritan Gift: Reclaiming the American Dream Amidst Global Financial Chaos*, I. B. Tauris, London and New York, 2009
A convincing treatment of the problems with "hero" leadership.

Jaworksi, Joseph *Synchronicity: The Inner Path of Leadership*, Berrett-Koehler, San Francisco, 1996
Profound messages about organisational learning and an inspiring account of the author's personal journey.

Johnstone, Keith *Impro: Improvisation and the Theatre*, Bloomsbury Methuen, London, 1981
Sets out helpful ideas about audiences responding to drama—has something to offer about influence between leaders and followers, and especially the role status plays in that context.

Kahane, Adam *Power and Love: A Theory and Practice of Social Change*, Berrett-Koehler, San Francisco, 2010
Makes a compelling case for the importance of combining love and power, just as in using two legs to walk.

Kahane, Adam *Transformative Scenario Planning: Working Together to Change the Future*, Berrett-Koehler, San Francisco, 2012
Further develops Adam Kahane's ideas with large-scale practical applications.

Knight, Sue *NLP at Work: The Essence of Excellence*, 3rd Edition (People Skills for Professionals), Nicholas Brealey, London, 2009
Sue Knight's standard on the principles and practice of Neuro Linguistic Programming.

Korzybski, Alfred *Selections from Science and Sanity: An Introduction to Non-Aristotelian Systems and General Semantics*, Second Edition, Institute of General Semantics, Fort Worth, Texas, 2010
In 1933, Alfred Korzybski began the whole philosophy of neuro-linguistics, which has become both popular and much more fully developed since. This is an abridged version of his main work.

Kotter, John *Leading Change*, Harvard Business Review Press, Boston, MA, 2012
An authoritative, readable, and accessible account of leading change in organisations.

Lambert, Andrew *Nelson: Britannia's God of War*, Faber and Faber, London 2004
Explores the nature of Nelson's genius.

Lawley, James and Tomkins, Penny *Metaphors in Mind: Transformation Through Symbolic Modelling*, The Developing Company, Lisburn, 2000
The definitive account of David Grove's work around the power of metaphor in our lives.

Madrazo, Claudia and Senge, Peter *Being the Change: Building Communities of Collaboration and Co-inspiration for Systemic Change*, Academy for Systemic Change, November 13, 2011
Important paper on the connection between the change needed "out there" and the change within ourselves.

Owen, Harrison *Open Space Technology: A User's Guide*, 3rd Edition, Berrett-Koehler, San Francisco, 2008
Attractively straightforward guide to a powerful approach to complex conversations.

Pais, Abraham *Subtle is the Lord, The Science and the Life of Albert Einstein*, Oxford University Press, Oxford, 1982
Rightly regarded as the classic account of both the man and his work. Conveys a sense of the immense scale of his achievements, as well as his human strengths and weaknesses.

Palmer, Parker J. *The Courage to Teach: Exploring the Inner Landscape of a Teacher's Life*, Jossey-Bass, San Francisco, 2007
Makes the case for reconnecting who we are with what we do. Written in the context of teaching, but of much wider relevance.

Peck, Scott M. *The Road Less Travelled*, Arrow, London, 1983
Popular modern classic on love and spirituality from a psychology perspective. A full and profound read.

Pressfield, Steven *The War of Art: Break Through the Blocks and Win Your Inner Creative Battles*, Black Irish Entertainment, New York, 2002
Pithy advice about getting on with it and overcoming "the resistance" that holds us back from doing great work.

Pressfield, Steven *Turning Pro: Tap Your Inner Power and Create Your Life's Work*, Black Irish Entertainment, New York, 2012
Charts the course of transforming your passion into your profession.

Rae, Alastair I. M. *Quantum Physics: A Beginner's Guide*, Oneworld, Oxford, 2005
Accessible explanation of the principles of quantum physics.

Ramo, Joshua Cooper *The Age of the Unthinkable: Why the New World Order Constantly Surprises Us and What We Can Do About It*, Little, Brown, London, 2009
A thought-provoking, if not troubling, account of the problems facing the world.

Rand, Ayn *Atlas Shrugged*, Penguin, London, 2007
Sets out Ayn Rand's philosophy of objectivism in a (lengthy) fictional form.

Rooke, David and Torbert, William R. *Seven Transformations of Leadership*, Harvard Business Review, Cambridge, MA, April 2005
Presents a useful model of the developing maturity of leaders, especially as it relates to change.

Rosen, Sydney (editor) *My Voice Will Go with You: The Teaching Tales of Milton Erickson*, Norton, New York, 1982
Conveys a sense of Milton Erickson's approach as a groundbreaking hypnotherapist and much more, including his take on the predominance of unconscious behaviour and learning.

Satir, Virginia *Peoplemaking*, Souvenir Press, London, 1978
A classic on the challenges of family life (and not so irrelevant to organisations and teams)—down-to-earth and uplifting in equal measure. Just as valid now as when it was written in 1972.

Senge, Peter *The Fifth Discipline: The Art & Practice of the Learning Organisation* (Revised Edition), Random House, London, 2006
Influential and rounded treatment of the characteristics of learning organisations and the art of change, including the concept of "personal mastery" as a vital ingredient.

Senge, Peter, Ross, Richard B., Smith, Bryan, Roberts, Charlotte and Kleiner, Art *The Fifth Discipline Fieldbook: Strategies and Tools for Building a Learning Organisation*, Nicholas Brealey, London, 1994
Expands on the principles in The Fifth Discipline with much practical material.

Senge, Peter, Scharmer, C. Otto, Jaworski, Joseph, and Flowers, Betty Sue *Presence: Exploring Profound Change in People, Organisations, and Society*, Nicholas Brealey, London, 2005
An intimate look at a new theory about change and learning.

Smith, Adam *The Theory of Moral Sentiments*, Penguin, London, 2010
In a first contribution to the Scottish Enlightenment, Smith addresses matters of common humanity.

Smith, Adam, Skinner, Andrew (editor) *The Wealth of Nations: Books I–III*, Penguin, London, 1982
Smith, Adam, Skinner, Andrew (editor) *The Wealth of Nations: Books IV–V*, Penguin, London, 1999
In two volumes, Adam Smith's classic work on the nature and causes of economic success.

Snowden, Ruth *Jung—The Key Ideas*, Bookpoint, Abingdon, 2006
A useful summary of Jung's thinking.

Sullivan, Wendy and Rees, Judy *Clean Language: Revealing Metaphors and Opening Minds*, Crown House Publishing, Carmarthen, 2008
An accessible guide to working with the power of metaphor as a coaching or therapeutic technique.

Sun Tzu *The Art of War*, Filiquarian Publishing LLC, Minneapolis, MN, 2006
Thoughts on handling conflict with economy of effort.

Tolle, Eckhart *The Power of Now*, Hodder and Stoughton, London, 2005
A book about mindfulness and living in the present. Life-changing, potentially, if you can stand apart long enough from the "voice in your head" to realise it's not you. Otherwise, come back later.

Williamson, Marianne *A Return to Love: Reflections on the Principles of A Course In Miracles*, HarperCollins, London, 1996
Established Marianne Williamson as an authority on spiritual intelligence.

Acknowledgements

Immediate family carry by far the heaviest burden as the development and writing of a book proceeds, through the loss of time and energy that would otherwise be spent with them, and, in reality, they have little choice in the matter. To Catriona and our children, therefore, thank you, for your belief, especially. If ever a model of faith is needed, several may well be found in one's family.

On the broader canvas, I wish to thank those from whom I have gained so much in the way of learning and insight from their wisdom, either from their books, talks, programmes, and workshops, or in many cases, conversations over the years, or a combination of all of these. Chris Argyris, David Bohm, Wayne Dyer, Gene Early, Seth Godin, Charles and Liz Handy, Stuart Hepburn, Sue Knight, John Kotter, Peter Senge and everyone at the Society for Organisational Learning, David Shephard, Peter Thomson, and Marianne Williamson come to mind particularly. Others have contributed vital insights at key moments. These include, but are by no means limited to, Matthew Anderson, Jim Mather, Michael Sales, and Ken Symon.

Thank you to everyone at CeeD Scotland for being the catalyst for this book through your kind invitation to speak on leadership in November 2012. The journey truly began with the preparation of my talk for the CeeD business audience and my reflections on the response it received. Thank you also for your continuing interest and support.

A joy, not to mention relief, in bringing a book together is in that moment when other people begin to see its purpose and contribute their time and energy to help make a reality of it, taking it from a solo project to a team effort. To the professionals involved in various capacities, Janet Aiossa, Mark Bloom, Stewart Cunningham, Gillian Dick, Lynda Gillespie, Angie Gray, Doug Strachan, and especially Shelley Lieber, thank you.

I am very grateful to Professor Sir Jim McDonald, Principal of Strathclyde University, for making space in his famously busy schedule to contribute the Foreword.

Early readers play a vital role in developing something worthwhile and in articulating how that may be relevant to the world. You can see what they had to say at the beginning of the book. Thank you to you all.

In my experience, writing a book, certainly one of this kind, involves letting go of security, stepping into the unknown, and trusting that other people will keep you safe. Friends and associates everywhere are the foundation of the necessary confidence, as well as the partners in many helpful conversations. This book wouldn't exist without them, though they probably don't realise how much what they said mattered. It would be unwise to attempt to name all these people. You know who you are. Thank you.

All in all, to receive the generous support of other people is a humbling experience.

And finally, putting last what should really be first, thank you for reading my book. I hope the learning makes as much difference to you as it has to me.

About the Author

Dr David Fraser began his career in engineering, later developing a particular curiosity about how to handle the human side of working life effectively and intelligently—in short, how to bring more wisdom into the workplace. His first book, *Relationship Mastery: A Business Professional's Guide*, was published in 2010.

David's academic and business career has always been about excelling. After securing First Class Honours in Engineering and a PhD at Glasgow University, he rose rapidly through several engineering companies including Thales and BAE Systems to the role of Programme Director in the naval shipyards on the River Clyde in Glasgow, later going on to lead a number of new enterprise companies. He is a Chartered Engineer and has an MBA from Strathclyde University.

Sounds like a great record? Yes, but there have been challenges, and, of course, we learn more when things go wrong than when they go right, especially when people are involved and we have complex organisational problems to solve. In response, David has developed a systematic approach to leadership and interpersonal effectiveness, incorporating numerous well-researched insights.

David works with organisations and with individuals, transforming both their immediate results and their future potential. For more information, see www.drdavidfraser.com or email david@davidfraser.com.

David lives in Glasgow, Scotland, with his wife and three children. He sails, cycles, and walks on the hills when time permits.

Unless someone like you cares a whole awful lot, nothing is going to get better. It's not.

— Dr Seuss